CAMBRIDGE STUDIES IN PHILOSOPHY

Matter and sense
A critique of contemporary materialism

CAMBRIDGE STUDIES IN PHILOSOPHY

General editor D. H. MELLOR

Advisory editors J. E. J. ALTHAM, SIMON BLACKBURN, DANIEL DENNETT, MARTIN HOLLIS, FRANK JACKSON, JONATHAN LEAR, T. J. SMILEY, BARRY STROUD

Matter and sense

A critique of contemporary materialism

Howard Robinson
Lecturer in Philosophy, University of Liverpool

Cambridge University Press

CAMBRIDGE
LONDON   NEW YORK   NEW ROCHELLE
MELBOURNE   SYDNEY

CAMBRIDGE UNIVERSITY PRESS
Cambridge, New York, Melbourne, Madrid, Cape Town, Singapore, São Paulo, Delhi

Cambridge University Press
The Edinburgh Building, Cambridge CB2 8RU, UK

Published in the United States of America by Cambridge University Press, New York

www.cambridge.org
Information on this title: www.cambridge.org/9780521114745

First published 1982
This digitally printed version 2009

A catalogue record for this publication is available from the British Library

Library of Congress Catalogue Card Number: 82–1176

ISBN 978-0-521-24471-8 hardback
ISBN 978-0-521-11474-5 paperback

TO
MANCHESTER GRAMMAR SCHOOL
Sapere Aude

Contents

Acknowledgments

Over the long period during which I have been working to produce this slim volume I have received help from many people. They include Robert Kirk, David Owen, Jonathan Barnes, Ralph Walker and the members of his discussion group, and the editors of *Cambridge Studies in Philosophy*. Julia Annas read and commented on an earlier draft of the book *in toto*. Most especially I am grateful to John Foster, who has read and criticised almost every chapter at almost every stage of its development. I would also like to thank Mrs Stella Russell for her help with the typing.

H. M. R.

1

The materialist's problem and some non-reductive solutions

I INTRODUCTION

William James divided philosophers into two psychological types, the tender-minded and the tough-minded. One of the characteristics of the tough-minded is a disposition to believe in philosophical materialism, whilst the tender-minded prefer dualism or idealism. The epithets 'tender-minded' and 'tough-minded' are not meant as evaluations of the arguments used to defend the theories each type is inclined to adopt; rather they describe the temperaments which are prone to accept and defend those theories: they are a psychological not a rational evaluation. Despite their association with the tough-minded temperament, materialist theories have tended to get the worst of the argument a bout the nature of the mind, if we judge by influence on the history of philosophy. Plato and Aristotle, for example, have had a greater appeal for philosophers through the ages than have the epicureans or the atomists: Descartes's influence is much greater than Hobbes's. This has been so despite the influence on modern philosophy of the materialistically inclined physical sciences. James also classified the approach and doctrines normally labelled 'empiricist' as tough-minded, yet empiricists have tended not to be materialists. The modern philosopher most representative of traditional empiricism, Sir Alfred Ayer, can both declare that his only object of faith is science and express a reluctant pessimism about the possibility of a coherent materialist theory of the human mind.[1] One may be tempted to cynicism and suspect that otherwise hard-nosed philosophers become tender-minded when dealing with their own souls. However, the history of philosophy plainly shows that the problems facing the materialist do not reside principally in a temperamental resistance to his doctrines, but in the genuine difficulty of providing a plausible materialist account of consciousness and the subjective dimension. Even at the peak of Victorian

1 For the faith in science see Ayer, 1966, and for his pessimism about physicalism see Ayer, 1977: 24ff.

1

mechanistic materialism the fashionable scientific view was that it was an epiphenomenon, an idle by-product of the physical system, not integrable within it (see e.g. Huxley, 1893). They saw their way to eliminating it from the realm of explanation, leaving that free to be monopolised by physical science, but they saw no way of either eliminating it from their ontology or integrating it into their materialist picture. At least one modern philosopher, Thomas Nagel, has trod the path to materialism via a theory of scientific explanation, only to retreat, conceding that even animals possess a subjectivity that modern materialism cannot capture.[2]

The growth in influence and the popularisation of physical science has made the problem more urgent. The idea that science captures everything, except the centre of everyone's universe, his own conscious\ess, makes a laughing-stock of its claim to present a plausible world view. The literate public as a whole lacks Ayer's firmness of mind and cannot hold steadily to a divided ideology. If science cannot encompass the subjective then subjectivity becomes a door through which mystical, irrational and religious notions can enter and reassert themselves against the modern metaphysic of scientific realism. It is not surprising, therefore, that in recent years philosophers committed to the scientific world picture have renewed their efforts to settle the matter in the materialist's favour.

Materialist theories have achieved a new thoroughness. Sometimes this means that they have shown greater subtlety in trying to 'save the phenomena' than earlier materialists, but sometimes it has been shown in a more daring denial of what others take to be the phenomena. Contemporary theories usually take one of three forms. First, they may consist of attempts to show how statements about mental states can be analysed into statements which are about physical states. Second, they may contain the courageous and desperate denial that statements about states of consciousness refer to anything at all, all of them being false. Or third, they may attempt to show that materialism can accommodate irreducibly subjective psychical states without ceasing to be genuinely materialistic.

We shall consider all three approaches. The last represents the most appealing programme, for, if true, we could be materialists without sacrificing our basic intuitions about consciousness: it is the least reductive and least counterintuitive of the strategies. We shall,

2   For the initial physicalism see Nagel, 1965, and for the partially reformed man, Nagel, 1974.

therefore, consider it first, and the discussion of the others will follow naturally from it.

Our conclusion will be that the materialist has gained nothing by his modern sophistication, because none of his theories is successful, nor do any indicate a plausible way to success. On the question of materialism, the truth is represented by a holy alliance between the tender-minded and those tough-minded empiricists who push their theory towards phenomenalism, rather than towards physicalism. We shall not in this short essay discuss what alternative theory of mind is to be preferred. The task of refuting materialism is sufficiently urgent, varied and difficult to require a work to itself. Nor shall we pursue in great detail the consequences for modernistic views of the world of their failure to capture the primary facts of human existence. But, to carry the battle a little into the enemy's territory, the last chapter will discuss the concept of matter, and we shall find that the suspicion and reserve with which a certain sort of empiricist has regarded this concept is amply justified. The materialist perceives the mote in his brother's eye whilst ignoring the beam in his own.

2 THE NATURE OF THE PROBLEM

The first task is to explain why mind should constitute such a formidable problem for materialism.

When a neurologist investigates the mechanisms by which someone perceives or thinks, why should he not claim that the physical processes he is investigating are themselves the subject's perceiving and thinking?

Broadly speaking, two different but compatible answers have been given to this question and I shall be concerned almost entirely with one only of those answers. The answer with which I shall not on the whole be concerned originates with Franz Brentano (1973: 88ff). He pointed out that many or all mental states manifest *intentionality*; that is, they are characterised by reference to something beyond themselves. Thus, if I think of or want to climb the Eiffel Tower, my thought is characterised by something beyond itself, namely the Eiffel Tower: that tower exists metaphorically, but not literally, in my mind. If materialism is correct, my thought or desire is in my head; the Eiffel Tower, however, is certainly not. This feature of the mind's meaning, pointing or intending something beyond itself, is something which many philosophers have thought cannot be numbered among or reduced to normal physical relations.

3

Whether this contention is sound is not easy to decide. Whether intentionality can be treated behaviouristically, so that thinking of something can be cashed out in terms of dispositions, probably including verbal dispositions, or whether some conception of mental representation, analogous to written and spoken language, can be used to reduce such things to physical tokens, are questions which involve difficult and tortuous investigation. The difficulty of such discussions is not a reason for not pursuing them. The fact that they are likely to be inconclusive is a better reason. The fact that there are computers which can mimic intelligent behaviour, of a sort that normally involves thoughts.and purposes, more or less guarantees that there is at least a materialist analogue for intentionality. One might well suspect that whether one is prepared to accept such a materialist account as an *analysis* rather than an *analogue* will depend on something other than its ability to mirror the formal properties of intentionality. Some more basic appeal to intuition concerning the phenomena of mind will be needed to settle the matter.

It is such a direct appeal to the phenomena of mind that constitutes the second general objection to materialism. This second objection concerns the data of consciousness itself. It is quite simply that the materialist cannot within his system allow for consciousness. Ayer has expressed this by saying that the materialist must pretend that he is anaesthetised (1977: 125, quoting Ogden and Richards, *The Meaning of Meaning*).

The argument can be developed with the help of a thought experiment. Imagine that a deaf scientist should become the world's leading expert on the neurology of hearing. Thus, if we suppose neurology more advanced than at present, we can imagine that he knows everything that there is to know about the physical processes involved in hearing, from the ear-drum in. It remains intuitively obvious that there is something which this scientist will not know, namely *what it is like to hear*. The same problem can be set up by imagining investigations carried out on a Martian who possesses a sixth sense that we lack. No matter how much we discover about his nervous system, we will not discover what the experiences he had by that sense were like (unless, perchance, the machinery suggested that it resembled one of our five senses). No amount of new information about the physical process will amount to information about *what it is like* to possess the sense in question. 'What it is like' is the sense viewed from the standpoint of the subject. It is this subjective

4

element which presents a serious challenge to the materialist. The mentalist thinks of these subjective states as instances of peculiarly mental properties, such as *feeling-a-pain* or *sensing-redly*. It would seem that the materialist cannot do this and must find some other treatment for subjectivity. A behaviourist, for example, asserts that *what it is like* to hear is simply the disposition to react directly to sound stimuli and that this disposition is all that our deaf scientist lacks: he lacks no factual information about any sort of property or state.

This might seem very elementary and obvious. It is, but it is not unusual for philosophers to misunderstand the sort of problem posed by consciousness. A number of materialists have argued that provided that one does not reify sense contents, sensory experience constitutes no problem. The rationale of their view is as follows. They assume that the difficulty for materialism is supposed to arise from the fact that when someone sees something red (for example) he has a red sense content in his mind, but there is no appropriate red thing to be found in his brain; therefore the experience is not identical with any brain state and materialism is false. They therefore suggest that if one analyses perception in some other way than the act–mental object model – adverbially, for example, or intentionally, or by direct realism – the problem will not arise. This is the central argument in James Cornman's defence of 'adverbial materialism' (1971: 267-78). It is also the essence of Anthony Quinton's claim that objections to materialism rest on a simple mistake (1973: 333). Thomas Nagel, too, at one point thought that there was no objection to identifying my seeing the Mona Lisa with a brain state once one had ceased to search for an image of the Mona Lisa in the brain (1965: 343). Slightly more indirectly, Joseph Margolis uses the same strategy (1978: 213). He argues that states that exhibit intentionality can be analysed reductively in a functional manner, and that sense contents, though not intentional themselves, are 'suitably embedded' in intentional states and therefore 'must be "realized" in the same way simpler intentional states are' (that is, physically). He too, therefore, believes that sense contents, provided they are infected by intentionality, pose no problem for the materialist. Nor is it only those who analyse sense contents intentionally or adverbially who fall into this mistake. Don Locke, who is a direct realist, says that veridical perception constitutes no problem for materialism, because the only content of such experience is a physical and public entity (1971).

5

It is not difficult to see why these approaches are inadequate. It is undoubtedly true that a belief in sense contents which actually instantiate or present qualities is incompatible with most forms of materialism. So it is very plausible to claim that a refusal to reify the internal objects of sensory awareness is a *necessary* part of a materialist strategy. Following U. T. Place's attack on 'the phenomenological fallacy' (which is precisely the 'fallacy' of reifying sense contents) most materialists have made this point as a preliminary to developing the difficult part of their own account (1956).[3] But the philosophers mentioned above appear to think that this constitutes the whole of, or at least the major part of, a defence of materialism. From our elementary exposition of the problem it should be clear why this is not so. The deaf scientist lacks a subjective state which we have characterised as 'what it is like to hear'. It is this state which in the nature of the case can never be brought within scientific theory. This predicament is quite independent of whether the sensory states in question are analysed in an extensional act—object or an adverbial manner. Physical science is necessarily as silent on 'sensing redly' or primitive awareness relations with something red, as it is on red sense-data. Investigation of the brain and description of it in neurophysical terms can no more unearth a state of sensing or an awareness relation to some external thing than it can a sense content. Unless adverbial or direct realist locutions are subject to reductionist analyses, they fall just as far beyond the boundary of physicalist discourse as sense contents themselves.

The source of the mistake made by Cornman and the others is the combining of two approaches to sense experience, each of which is plausible by itself, but not in combination with the other. The first approach is to emphasise the supposed intentionally inexistent status of the internal objects of awareness. This leads some philosophers to think that one can discount any question about their ontological status.[4] The second is to consider the act of awareness in isolation from its object and to note that alone it has no definite scrutable properties. This manoeuvre resembles Hume's failure to introspect anything but the *objects* of his awareness. Considered together, the act and the object, each viewed in this way, have no specifiable and actual features. The object has features but is not actual; the mental

3 Wilson, 1979, argues that it is not possible to dereify the internal object of experience, but sees no reason why the having or apprehending of that object cannot be treated in a materialist way, without reductionism. The argument in the text shows why this is not possible.
4 For example, Anscombe, 1968. For a reply to this approach, see Robinson, 1974.

act is actual but has no introspectable features. Therefore, how can they be known by introspection to exhibit features which are incompatible with materialism? But this strategy is misconceived, for it is not possible both to separate act and object in this way and to dereify the object. If one takes a simple act–internal object approach, then the existence of the object and its features must be taken seriously. If, on the other hand, one dereifies the object, it becomes an 'adverbial' feature of the act and the act therefore has the scrutable mental property of being *of-something-F*. Furthermore, even in the case where the object is detached from the act (and in direct realism the object is extramental) the act still has the mental feature of being an awareness relation: this is a state entirely unknown to physical ontology. Unless some reductive account of it is provided, an unanalysed relation of awareness will be emergent with respect to any physical characterisation.

It is not difficult to prove that Cornman *et al.* are involved in a mere conjuring trick. Let us suppose it legitimate both to dereify the internal object of awareness and to deny that the act possessed any introspectable features. It would follow that there was no introspectable and real difference between having an experience and not having one: that is, from the viewpoint of the conscious subject there is no difference between being conscious and not being conscious, except in terms of something which is not existent. This is manifestly absurd and amounts to a denial of the existence of consciousness. Perhaps the mistake made is slightly less bizarre than this. Perhaps the idea is that one can tell introspectively the difference between having an experience and not doing so, or between having *this* experience and having *that* one, but one cannot tell what that difference consists in. However, it is plain that one can tell the difference in terms of the object of experience. One can tell that one is having an experience because one has an object of awareness, and by what that object is one can tell what sort of experience one is having. The notion of *having something as an object of experience* is not, *prima facie*, a physical notion; it does not figure in any physical science.[5] *Having something as an object of experience* is the same as the subjective feel or the *what it is like* of experience. Another way of stating the

5   M. E. Levin, 1979, presents himself as a topic-neutral reductionist whilst helping himself to such notions as *being aware of x* and *intuiting x*. In ch. 3.7 we shall see that he makes no better case than the philosophers we are criticising at the moment. Smart, on the other hand, gives a topic-neutral analysis of the internal object of experience. We shall see in ch. 3.8 what deep water this lands him in.

7

materialist's problem is to say that he must explain in a physicalist way what it is for someone to have something as an object of experience.

3 DAVIDSON'S DUAL ASPECT THEORY

One well established materialist tradition is happy with the irreducible nature of subjectivity and mental states and properties. This is the dual aspect theory. The dual aspect theory has not received much explicit discussion in recent years because of a tendency not to regard it as a genuine form of materialism. This reservation has three main grounds. First, it is doubtful whether an object which possesses both mental and physical properties is a material object in the strict sense. It is natural to define an object by reference to its properties. Does not the dual aspect theory make man a mental object just as much as a material one? Second, one of the two main motives behind modern materialist theories is the desire to provide a total world description in terms of physical science. The picture of the world as a great machine (with some random elements) on to which are stuck, in the appropriate places, some extra and non-physical states spoils this original architectonic. These states cannot be drawn into the web of physical science, for they are of a wholly different nature. In Herbert Feigl's phrase, they are 'nomological danglers' tied to physical reality by arbitrary correlation laws of their own (1958). The idea of this radical discontinuity of properties is hardly less offensive than dualism. Third, it presents problems for the unity of scientific theory considered as explanatory as well as descriptive. Is the presence of mental properties supposed to exert a causal influence and thus to produce emergent psycho-physical and psychological laws not inferable from physical science? If the answer is that the mental presence does produce such emergence then some of the most objectionable features of dualism reappear. How is the interaction between mental and physical aspects to be understood? The unity of physical science is destroyed. But if the mental does not affect the operation of physical laws, and mechanism is true, is the mental aspect not then epiphenomenal, which is profoundly counterintuitive?

Despite these problems, there has developed a fashionable form of materialism which appears to be a version of the dual aspect theory. The proponents of this modern version of the theory do not express themselves by saying that all *substances* are physical whilst some of

8

their properties are not (though they would presumably not deny this) but rather claim that all *events* are physical, though some possess an irreducibly psychical aspect. This formulation stems from considering the problem of materialism via the question 'Are all events physical events?' This emphasis on events is inspired by a novel theory of event identity. Nagel is generally credited with originating the theory, (1965: 343ff), though its further development and use are associated with Donald Davidson (1969). We shall be investigating its merits as a general account of event identity in the final section of the chapter. All that need be stated at the moment are the bare bones of the theory; namely that event *a* is identical with event *b* if and only if *a* and *b* have exactly the same causal relations. Nagel calls this 'theoretical identity' because it enables one to make identifications between events on different theoretical levels. For example, some water's boiling is said to be the same event as the agitation of the molecules of some H_2O because these two events have the same causes and the same effects. Various philosophers have taken up this general theory of event identity and applied it to the relation between mental and physical events. This approach has generated the most influential contemporary forms of avowedly non-reductive materialism. (I say *avowedly* non-reductive because as our discussion progresses we shall discover that the term 'reductionism' has many senses and that some philosophers are confused about what it is they are trying to avoid. Chapter 2 is devoted largely to showing that certain theories are more reductionist than they pretend to be.)

We saw above that the dual aspect theory may or may not be held in conjunction with a belief in mechanism — that is, with the theory that, in so far as a physical event has a causal explanation (some might be random and have no cause), that explanation will be in terms of necessary and sufficient *physical* conditions. The mechanist denies that non-physical influences ever cause a physical system to do things which are not determined by physical necessity. We also remarked above that the combination of the dual aspect theory and mechanism seems necessarily to entail that the mental aspect is an epiphenomenon, for mechanism ensures that everything the body does can be fully causally explained without reference to the mental. The mental is therefore an idle by-product of the physical system. One of the striking things about those philosophers who bring the causal theory of event identity to bear on the philosophy of mind is that they espouse mechanism and a sort of dual aspect theory whilst

9

denying epiphenomenalism. They are, they claim, interactionists. One of their number, Davidson, believes mechanism to be necessarily true on the grounds that causal explanations must be strictly nomological but explanations by reference to mental states cannot be strictly nomological: the mental is anomalous (1971). It follows that every event which has a causal explanation (i.e. is not random) has a complete physical explanation. Christopher Peacocke, who follows Davidson's general approach to event identity, does not involve himself in doctrines concerning the anomalism of the mental. He, like most materialists, thinks that the achievement of science so far makes it unreasonable to believe that some external non-physical influence is necessary to give a causal explanation of the behaviour of bodies (1979). For him, therefore, mechanism is an empirical hypothesis.

Whatever the motives of these philosophers in adopting mechanism, it must surely place them in the same position as others who before them have tried to combine property dualism and mechanism, namely the predicament of being epiphenomenalists about the mental. This appears to be guaranteed by the causal sufficiency of the physical. Appreciation of this point is a principal reason why materialists indulge in reductive theories of mental predicates, for on those theories mentalistic language becomes only a special way of talking about physical states and behaviour, thus having nothing for its reference beyond the great physical machine: the mind is then not an epiphenomenon, but a part or physical aspect of the physical. Without such reduction epiphenomenalism appears to be an inevitable consequence of mechanism.

Davidson and Peacocke claim that one can avoid epiphenomenalism by identifying mental events with physical events, whilst accepting that mental and physical properties and states are quite different. The argument is ingenious but sophistical. They admit that any plausible theory of mind must allow for the interaction both ways of mind and body. The influence of body on mind is compatible with mechanism; it is the loss of the influence of mind on body that we fear may follow. Such influence seems naturally to be expressed in the thesis that mental events sometimes cause physical events. Davidson affirms this thesis, but allows it a completely unnatural interpretation (1971: 99f). He asserts (for reasons we will investigate later) that every mental event is also a physical event, although mental states and properties are not identical with any physical states or prop-

10

erties. Hence mental events can cause physical events, because they themselves are physical events. Thus, if my feeling a pain in the leg is identical with brain event B, and brain event B causes my hand to reach for my leg, then (the event of) my feeling a pain caused me to reach to my leg.

However, the form of interactionism so generated is entirely empty. Indeed to call it 'interaction' seems disingenuous, for it remains the case that the mentality of the event played no part in bringing about its effect and therefore is itself inert and epiphenomenal. Furthermore, had the mental been absent no difference would have resulted. Thus if brain event B or one just like it had occurred in just the same physical context but without its mental aspect, the same behaviour would have followed in virtue of natural law. If we are allowed to call this 'interaction', then by parity of argument one can prove that inert gases interact with other gases.

Call any event which takes place in an atmosphere containing some inert gas an 'inert gas event'. Call any event taking place in an atmosphere containing some active gas an 'active gas event'. Now the striking of a match in a sufficiently large sample of our normal air will be both an inert gas event and an active gas event. It will, we can assume, be followed by the match's catching fire, which will also be both sorts of event. We therefore have an inert gas event which *causes* something to happen – indeed causes an active gas event. Does this prove that there are no inert gases because inert gases really interact with things? Of course it does not, for no inert gas or inert gas property played any role in bringing about the flame. If the small amount of inert gas in that atmosphere had been removed, the flame would still have burned and that neither more nor less brightly. The inert gas event has causal power, but not *qua* inert gas event: the gas is inert, an epiphenomenon beyond the drama of ignition. The mental is just as epiphenomenal as the inert gases are inert and in exactly the same way. Interaction involves the relevance of the object (e.g. argon or mind) or its states and properties to the causal relations into which it enters. Something must make a causal contribution to avoid being inert or epiphenomenal. The Davidsonian claim that mental events make a contribution, when combined with the admission that the mental state does not is fundamentally misleading. That this is how we understand causal interaction is shown by the fact that it is the lack of this type of contribution which justifies us in saying that certain gases are inert. The fact that they are present at the occurrence

11

of certain causally efficacious events is not sufficient to make it true to say that they interact with anything.

There are within Davidson's own apparatus the resources for explaining why his theory is not interactionist and why mind is comparable to an inert gas. Davidson (1967: 697) distinguishes between

(1) *a* causes *b*

and

(2) *a* causally explains *b*.

(1) is extensional, because its truth-value is unaffected by the manner of reference to *a* and *b*. (2) can be treated extensionally, but is fundamentally intensional, because causal explanation follows laws and laws link events under certain aspects. Thus (2) can be filled out in either of the following ways:

(3) *a* under some description or other causally explains *b* under some description or other;

(4) *a* under F causally explains *b* under G.

(4) will be true if there is a natural law roughly of the form 'All FS cause GS.' The inert gas event of the striking causes, as in (1), the active gas event of ignition: it also causally explains it under some description or other, as in (3), for that very event can be described in terms which invoke the active features present. But if we substitute 'occurring in an atmosphere containing inert gas' for 'F', then we shall not get a true substitution into (4), for the event under that description causally explains nothing. This is what the inertness of inert gases comes to. An exactly parallel argument works for the supposed interaction of mental and physical on Davidson's scheme. A mental event *a* extensionally causes a physical event *b*: it also causally explains it under some physical description which is supposed to apply to it, as in (3). But if we substitute the mental description for 'F', we will fail to find a true version of (4). Therefore we have a clear demonstration that the mental is inert in just the same way as inert gases are inert, and that interaction depends not upon some extensional causal relation but upon the intensional explanatory relevance of that feature in virtue of which the objects are supposedly interacting.

I initially asserted that Davidson's theory made the mental epiphenomenal because it had the consequence that, had the mental been absent but the physical circumstances remained the same, the same physical consequences would have followed. The argument I have employed has not called on this counterfactual. In chapter 2 we shall see, in the course of a discussion of supervenience, that Peacocke denies that this counterfactual represents a real possibility. We shall also see that he is wrong and that this objection too holds against the Davidsonian pattern for interaction.

4 EVENT IDENTITY

Although we have shown that the causal criterion of event identity does not help the materialist, we have not actually refuted it as a theory about events. Indeed while that theory remains unrefuted it will still remain possible for the materialist who combines mechanism and dual aspect theory to say that mental events are identical with physical events and that, therefore, mental events cause physical ones. It has been proved that what this means is not what it normally means and that they are using a systematically misleading form of words. Nevertheless, the air will be clearer if we can refute the theory of event identity that underpins this sophistry. Moreover, we shall find that the correct theory of event identity − namely one based on the identity of properties − prevents one from holding a mental−physical identity theory in conjunction with a non-reductive account of mental properties. This latter conclusion is just what one would expect, for, at first sight, a non-reductionist theory of mental properties and states would seem to suggest that mental and physical events are not identical: if mental property M and physical property P are quite separate *qua* properties, then how can the coming-to-be-instantiated of M be the same event as the coming-to-be-instantiated of P?

The suggestion that the individuation of events via properties is the natural way to proceed is one to which we shall return. First we must consider the theory of event identity which the Davidsonians employ. They argue that events *a* and *b* are identical if and only if every event which is a cause of *a* is also a cause of *b*, and every event which is a cause of *b* is a cause of *a*; and every event which is an effect of *a* is also an effect of *b*, and every event which is an effect of *b* is also an effect of *a*. In short, sameness of event is solely a function of sameness of causes and effects (Davidson, 1969: 231; Peacocke, 1979: 117-18).

The causal criterion is intended to perform the same task for events as spatio-temporal continuity does for bodies. That is, it is a criterion of identity and not an account of what an event is (Davidson, 1969:

13

225). There are two reasons why this must be so and why the criterion cannot pose as an account of what events essentially are. First, it would be vacuous as such an account. To say that an event is what is caused by and causes other events is circular: nothing is there said about what an event *is*. Second, it would be plainly false, for there could be a world in which there was only one event − say a blue flash − and that event had neither cause nor effect. Indeed, there may be such events in our world for all we know. These considerations show that the 'stuff and guts' of events do not consist in their causal relations: there must be *something that happens*, and to characterise this one must resort to properties and their coming to be, continuing to be or ceasing to be instantiated at certain locations.

This exhibits a crucial disanalogy with the spatio-temporal continuity criterion for the individuation of bodies. One could roughly define a body as something which occupies space: it is an area characterised by solidity, or some form of resistance to penetration. It follows naturally from this account of what a body is that one should individuate bodies at a given time by reference to the different areas of space they occupy and through time by reference to the spatial paths they follow through that time. The spatio-temporal continuity criterion is merely an extension or extrusion through time of body as we conceive it statically − i.e. of the notion of a space occupier. This is what one would expect: that is, one would expect a criterion for individuation to follow necessarily from the essence of the thing individuated. But the essence of events consists in the properties involved in them: they are both (a) essential to something's happening at all and (b) what constitutes *what* has happened. One might reasonably expect, therefore, that a criterion for the individuation of events make essential reference to the properties that constitute those events. Not merely is this not so on the causal criterion, but, worse, the feature chosen to constitute the individuation of events is one which is not an essential feature of events as such, as we have seen from the fact that it is possible to imagine events without either causes or effects. It is surely bizarre, if not worse, to suggest that the criterion for *a* and *b* being the same F is some feature which is entirely accidental to being F. Therefore, some criterion statable in terms of properties is the intuitively natural account of the individuation of events. So it is not surprising that the brunt of the argument for the causal criterion consists in attempting to show that no coherent and acceptable version of a property-based criterion can be stated; in which case the causal criterion gets by as a *pis aller*.

The fact is that the case for the property criterion has been handled in a strange way. Jaegwon Kim initially stated it in terms of a triple of subjects, times and properties (1966, 1976). Thus an event consists of some particular a's coming, remaining or ceasing to be F at time t: b's coming, remaining or ceasing to be G at time t' will be the same event as the former if and only if $a = b$, $t = t'$ and F = G. Unfortunately, there are more instantiated properties than there are events. Putting the same problem in a slightly different way, the same event can fall under a variety of descriptions. We do not want a particular object's becoming coloured to be a different event from its becoming red, if red is the colour it becomes, nor Caesar's being stabbed to be a different event from his being killed, nor a log's rolling to be different from its rolling slowly, although in all three cases we have pairs of differing properties.

One of Kim's reactions to this problem was to distinguish between intrinsic and extrinsic characterisations of events (1976: 166-7). Thus, intrinsically the Caesar event was a stabbing, but it is extrinsically a killing in view of its causal connection with later events – i.e. Caesar's heart stopping. Instead of pursuing the task of distinguishing the intrinsic from the extrinsic in a rigorous manner, Kim is sidetracked by a concern with causal explanation and decides that if different descriptions of what appears to be the same event bring into play different causal explanations, then we have different events (1976: 169). This constitutes a hopeless ontological profligacy, for almost any different description opens the way to a different causal explanation. What explains why Caesar was stabbed (as opposed to strangled etc.) will be different from what explains why he was killed; the explanation of something's being coloured may be different from that of its being red; and the explanation of the log's rolling may be different from that of its rolling slowly. He claims that one of the events – e.g. the slow rolling – may include others – e.g. the rolling – but they are still different.

Kim's first thought was better than his second. The attempt to provide a different event for every explanandum is a mistake, whereas that of providing a proper intrinsic description is not. Talk of events 'under a description' instead of talk of properties, while not strictly wrong, is liable to mislead. It suggests that the properties involved in events are somehow language dependent and that

15

therefore what 'really' happens depends on what we choose to say about it. A more robustly realist approach to the properties in the world is more helpful. The strategy that the property theorist should adopt, therefore, is to take a firmly realist approach to properties *in rebus* and to provide an account of how a variety of descriptions can be ways of referring to the same properties. In this way he can explain how a variety of descriptions can be true of the coming to be, ceasing to be or remaining instantiated of a particular property. This sort of realism is something which comes naturally to us in the case of objects. We are quite happy to think of a variety of descriptions of varying degrees of specificity as referring to the same object. No-one would think of applying Kim's procedure here. For example, we are clear that the hard, brown, wooden table is the same object as the table. If we tried to apply Kim's treatment of events to substances we would say that there were several objects here, some included in others. Thus the hard, brown, wooden table includes, though is not identical with, the wooden table, the brown thing, the coloured table, the hard brown item of furniture etc. We do not feel obliged to multiply substances in this way, and, if possible, we should not multiply events. There is no relevant distinction to be made between substances and events in terms of differences of explanation, for why I have a wooden table might have a different explanation from why it is coloured, just as why the log is rolling slowly might have a different explanation from why it is rolling. Nor is there any greater difficulty in recognising that the slow event and the rolling are the same event than there is in recognising that it is the table which is the brown thing. Rollings must have speeds as tables must have colour; and they must have precise speeds (e.g. 2·76 m.p.h.) from which whether it is slow or fast etc. can be deduced. We know what specific types of feature a generic event or substance must have, and we do not multiply entities by altering the specificity with which they are characterised. Nor does one multiply by adding part to whole. There is not the table, its leg and one of the atoms in its leg. All these things do exist, but not in addition to each other. The inclusion relation by which Kim seeks to deal with added specificity really fits the part—whole relation. This is equally true of events as of substances: there was not the Battle of Britain in addition to the Second World War. Whether the sum of the parts is identical with the whole or whether the 'is' of composition is different from identity is not something we need investigate here. My sole point is that one need not treat events in any less intuitive a way than we treat substances. If one believes that some possible scientific theory could list all the objects that compose the physical world on its most basic microscopic level, such that all more macroscopic objects are simply composed of these, one can also believe that the basic events in the world are those involving changes of the properties specified in that theory.

With some trepidation, I shall end this chapter by attempting to state an adequate form of the property criterion for event identity. Perhaps it can be regimented in the following way. First there are two conditions necessary for object a's being F at t being identical with b's being G at t':

(1) $a = b$;
(2) $t = t'$.

These conditions take care of the objects and the times. The problem lies in dealing with the properties. I suggest that at least one of the following conditions must hold:

(3) 'F' and 'G' refer to or invoke the same property.

One instance of (3) is when 'F' and 'G' have the same sense, but there are other cases. For example, 'the colour of the sky', 'the colour of the sea' and 'blue' all refer to the colour blue and therefore the predicates formed simply from these expressions can be said to invoke that property. The two descriptions, given their sense, do so contingently, and the name given its sense does so analytically.

Kim's system goes this far and no further. The following disjuncts have no place in his theory:

(4) The F event constitutes the G event, given the context.

There are at least two types of context, namely conventional and causal: saying 'I do' counts as marrying given a context defined by English law; and stabbing Caesar constituted killing him, given that the stabbing caused his death. The extra disjuncts towards which the discussion above leads are:

(5) The F event is the G event under a more specific description: that is, it specifies some determinate feature from a determinable range that G events standardly possess.

This is the relation between 'slow rolling' and 'rolling'.

(6) The F event is constituted by the same set of micro-events as the G event.

(6) generally includes (5). Thus the log's rolling and its rolling slowly will be the same event because exactly the same set of events characterised on the microscopic level constituted both events. This

17

parallels the way in which it suffices for John's dining table and John's favourite piece of furniture to be the same object that they both be constituted by the same microscopic entities. Indeed, it is plain that when 'two' events are constituted by the same micro-events their subjects will be constituted by the same micro-objects. However, (6) will not always do (5)'s work, for some events may not have micro-event components. For example, the most microscopic events and many mental events do not possess event parts. (6) can be be varied to give a necessary condition of event identity, namely that if events are identical it cannot be the case that they have different micro-constituents.

It might seem that a theory with four disjuncts is somewhat *ad hoc*, but this is not so. What the variety of alternatives shows is the number of different ways we have of talking about the same events, just as there are alternative ways of describing objects. What the disjuncts all have in common is that all exhibit ways in which the same happening, characterised by a property, can be referred to by expressions which do not possess that property as their sense: there can be many ways of referring to the same property-instance, just as there can be many ways of referring to the same substance.

We have already shown that Davidson's theory of event identity does not, even if true, help the materialist. However, if the views developed in this section are sound then that criterion is false. If we adopt the property criterion, the coming-to-be-instantiated of a mental property and the coming-to-be-instantiated of a physical one will be the same event only if the properties are related as outlined above. It is fairly obvious that they will not meet those standards if no reductive analysis is given of mental predicates, and the various forms of reductive materialism I shall be considering below do try to make them fit one of the four models. For example, taken non-reductively mental predicates are not synonymous with physical ones, though Carnap's physicalism and some forms of analytical behaviourism claim that they are (Carnap, 1934; see also ch. 3.1). Nor do they appear to refer to the same property while not being synonymous: there is no intuitive difficulty in seeing how blue can qualify as the colour of the sky, but why some brain property should count as, for example, a pain would need explanation. This explanation is what the topic-neutral analysis of mental discourse attempts to provide (see ch. 3.4). Thus mental and physical events are not identical under (3) without reductionism. Nor does a physical event

18

count as a mental one in an appropriate causal or conventional context, unless we give something like a functionist analysis of mental predicates (see ch. 2.7); thus (4) is excluded if we do not resort to reduction. Nor are psychological expressions merely more or less precise ways of referring to physical events. (In this case I can think of no form of reductionism that has adopted the approach.) Nor are mental events 'made from' physical ones, as macroscopic from microscopic. This picture is perhaps the one adopted by those who talk of 'molar behaviour' as being constructed from biochemical events (Wilkes, 1978), or who compare the mental—physical relation to that between individuals and nations (see ch. 2.3). Perhaps it counts in favour of our approach to event identity that conditions (3) to (6) more or less mirror different reductive approaches to the mind. It shows, at least, that they implicitly possess an understanding of the problem similar to mine.

2

Supervenience and reduction

I SUPERVENIENCE AND NECESSITY: THE OPTIONS

The concept of reduction has always played an important part in the discussion of materialist theories. To some extent it is a 'boo' word, signifying that the materialist is adopting a counterintuitive position — one which involves claiming that mind is other than it seems. For this reason the philosophers we have been discussing so far deny that they are reductionists. They say that the mental is not *reducible* to the physical, although it *supervenes* upon it. The purpose of this chapter is to investigate the fashionable concept of supervenience and to see how, if at all, it differs from reduction.

It is convenient to start this investigation by picking up an unfinished line of argument from our discussion of interaction and epiphenomenalism (see ch. 1.3). One criterion of whether an event or state is epiphenomenal and does not interact with other things is whether its absence would have had causal consequences, *ceteris paribus*. We showed that mental events were epiphenomenal on Davidson's and Peacocke's theory without recourse to this criterion: we showed that *a* interacts with *b* to produce *c* only if *a* causally explains *c*, whereas on their theory the occurrence of mental states causally explains nothing. However, reversion to the former criterion is a good place to begin a discussion of supervenience. It serves this purpose because the question 'What would have happened if mental states had been absent and other things had remained the same?' will only have application if it makes sense to suggest that mental states might have been absent while physical states remained the same. But materialists of the school we are discussing do not allow that a situation might be reduplicated physically without being reduplicated mentally. They do not believe that there could be a robot which reduplicated human physical states but lacked mental ones; it is not merely empirically impossible, it is impossible *tout court*. This, they say, is because the mental *supervenes upon* the physical.[1] Quine ex-

1 Davidson, 1971: 88, and 1973: 716-17; Peacocke, 1979: 116-24. Peacocke employs the closely

20

presses this idea by saying that 'there is no mental difference without a physical difference' (Quine, 1977: 187, quoted in Healey, 1978-9). Of course, if the counterfactual we desire is to be excluded, it is not enough that there *is* no mental difference without a physical difference; it must be that there *cannot* be a mental difference without a physical one. This leaves us with a question about the nature of the necessity which generates this 'cannot'. The origin of the term 'supervenience' lies in Moore's account of the relation of ethical to natural properties (Davidson, 1973: 717). One might think that the rationale of supervenience in Moore's moral theory was sufficiently obscure for it not to throw much illumination on the present case. Davidson does refer to this origin as if the analogy were helpful (1973: 717). The connexion involved is presumed to be stronger than the necessity of physical law, as normally conceived, for if it were empirical in this way we could conceive of its not holding and thereby describe a possible world in which our counterfactual was true. On the other hand, it is not meant to be as strong as logical necessity, where that involves *a priori* entailment from physical to mental. If it were such logical necessity, a full description of the physical situation in physical terms would entail the appropriate mental description *a priori*. This *a prioricity* would be possible only if there was a strong connexion in meaning between mental and physical predicates, and this would involve some form of analytical reductionism, which is supposedly disavowed. Quine simply asserts that the supervenience of everything on physics is a sort of regulative principle of physics, though he hardly manages to explain how or why this should be so; at best we might grant that it was a methodological rule of thumb (1977: 192, quoted in Healey, 1978-9). Another sort of necessity, sometimes called 'metaphysical necessity', has come into vogue. This sort of necessity is, I think, normally associated with the *a posteriori* necessity which Saul Kripke discovers in what had previously been called contingent identities. Kripke has argued that if $a = b$ then necessarily $a = b$, whether a and b be particulars or natural kinds. From this it seems natural to infer that if the mental is identical with the physical then it is so necessarily (Kripke, 1971, 1972). There is no real possibility that they might not have been identical: therefore they could not vary independently. (Kripke himself does not think that the mental is identical with the physical, so the question of whether it necessarily is so does not arise for him.)

connected concept of *realisation*.

21

The fundamental contention of this chapter is that the concept of supervenience involves a sense of 'necessity' which hovers or oscillates between the metaphysical and the logical. I shall argue that the logical is the only one which will serve the materialist's purposes and, therefore, that the concept of supervenience is quite useless to non-reductive materialism.

2 PEACOCKE AND KRIPKE

Peacocke attempts to use Kripkean metaphysical necessity as a way of expressing the supervenience relation. He argues that it is not a 'real metaphysical possibility' that the physical state upon which a mental state supervenes should occur in the absence of that state, or vice versa (1979: 125). His reason seems to be as follows. Consider the hypothesis that c-fibre firing is identical with pain. 'c-fibres' denotes a natural kind of stuff; therefore, if their firing has this mental aspect, then it necessarily does so, just as, for Peacocke, water necessarily has the property of being essential to humans. Therefore, the hypothesis that c-fibre firing might not be identical with pain does not express a real possibility. To avoid this problem, he says, one might try to characterise c-fibres qualitatively instead of designating them rigidly. For instance, though water could not have failed to be H_2O, something qualitatively like water could be made up of different constituents, so something qualitatively just like c-fibres might be different in respect of its mental concomitant (Peacocke, 1979: 128). This follows Kripke's own recommended way of characterising what is legitimate in the supposed contingency of some identities (1971: 158ff). Thus, one will come up with the hypothesis that it is a real possibility that 'strands of grey fibrous cells of such and such a shape are stimulated and pain is absent'. Of this Peacocke says that it is true 'since presumably strands of grey ... etc. are not necessarily c-fibres' (1979: 130). Peacocke's contention, it seems, is that it is not possible to specify what physical state one is referring to in a sufficiently exact way as to succeed in referring to the relevant physical state that obtains in the world, while at the same time leaving it open whether that state is the sort of state (or state of a sort of stuff) that could possibly lack a mental aspect. Thus, if you say 'grey fibres ... etc.' you might not be describing c-fibres, but if you say 'c-fibres' it is no longer possible that what you refer to might have lacked any of the properties nature has in fact given it.

Even leaving aside the contentiousness of Kripke−Putnam doctrines about necessity as applied to natural kinds, this argument will not suffice. Peacocke's treatment of each horn of the dilemma is defective, though in essentially the same way. First, it is difficult to see how the mental aspect of c-fibre activity could be essential to it if c-fibres are regarded as natural kinds whose essence is revealed by science, for their mental life is nowhere referred to in their physical scientific characterisation. No information concerning their chemical composition will essentially involve reference to mental events; thus the latter have no part of their real essence as physical processes. This point is reinforced if the mental is anomalous, for no scientific characterisation of them, which must be in terms of scientific, nomic properties, will involve a mental, anomic proclivity. Second, a qualitative description of c-fibres that says everything about them that could be said about them in physical theory is, *ex hypothesi*, sufficient to characterise the type of physical state in which one is interested, and it will not involve the ascription of mental properties, for they do not figure in physical theory. So, given that physical theories do not mention mental properties and given that they say everything one needs to know about the physical aspect of the c-fibres to individuate them among physical things, it must be possible to give a qualitative characterisation of c-fibres which is, on the one hand, rich enough to pick out accurately the sort of physical thing we are interested in, and, on the other, involves no necessary commitment to the presence of the mental. This can be done by saying of c-fibres all and only what an adequate physical theory would say of them. These considerations obviously have no special relevance to the case of c-fibres and pain: if they are sound they can be generalised to the physical system as a whole.

Peacocke's claim that it is impossible to specify what exactly the physical system is without implicitly involving the mental element and that it is therefore impossible to conceive that there should be a system physically just like the actual world yet lacking mentality, is, therefore, false. We have no reason to think that a humanoid robot is not a real metaphysical possibility; and the type of necessity involved in supervenience cannot be analysed in terms of Kripke's *a posteriori* necessity.

Given this conclusion we can reinforce our claim from chapter 1 that the dual aspect theory with mechanism must lead to epiphenomenalism. We have shown that the supposition that the mental might have been absent whilst the world remained physically the same expresses a metaphysical possibility. Given mechanism, it follows that no physical event in the world would have been altered by this. It would, therefore, follow that the mental is an idle epiphenomenon.

3 DISAVOWING REDUCTION: SIGNS OF CONFUSION

I have said that all the philosophers we are at present discussing claim not to be reductionists, but that there is a certain obscurity about what they mean by this. Peacocke is alone, I think, in claiming that, not merely are mental predicates irreducible, but that subjectivity is a *sui generis* non-physical phenomenon (1979: 172-3). If what has been said above is correct, it is difficult to see how he could successfully combine this view with the theory that the mental supervenes on the physical. However, he does at times succumb to the temptation to employ a more reductionist model of supervenience. It is expressed in an analogy. The analogy is with the relation between individuals and nations. By following up this analogy we shall find ourselves in the middle of the confusion that prevails about the exact sense of the term 'reduction'. Once we have sorted this out it will become clear in what sense supervenience is a form of reduction.

Peacocke takes it to be obvious that statements about nations supervene 'upon psychological and semantic statements about individual citizens of nations' (1979: 122). This analogy, though typical of those used to explain supervenience, surely raises the spectre of reductionism. Davidson, defending his own very similar form of materialism from the charge of reductionism, pleads as follows. 'Such a bland monism, unbuttressed by correlating laws or conceptual economies, does not seem to merit the term "reductionism"; in any case it is not apt to inspire the nothing-but reflex ("Conceiving of the *Art of Fugue* was nothing but a complex neural event" and so forth)' (1971: 88). The analogy between nations and individuals is precisely apt to inspire that reflex: it is very natural to say that nations are *nothing but* people in a complex organisation.

It is obvious that we shall have to become much clearer about supervenience and about reduction before we can decide whether the former is a species of the latter. Philosophers who espouse supervenience but eschew reduction have a very strong concept of reduction. What they are eschewing is the claim that mental descriptions can be translated or paraphrased into physical ones. What they intend to disown, therefore, are such programmes as analytical behaviour-

24

ism or Carnap's brand of physicalism. It is to emphasise the impossibility of such an intensional equivalence between mental and physical descriptions that they deny that there is even an extensional equivalence between types of mental and physical states: if there are no contingent laws there certainly cannot be translation of mental into physical descriptions, for translatability entails co-extensiveness. At first sight there are two sorts of reduction. First, there is the translation reduction just mentioned: second, there is the 'nothing-but' reduction illustrated by the relation between individuals and nations, or between atoms and macroscopic objects. Some philosophers seem to regard this second sort as reduction, whereas others seem to regard it as materialism without reduction. We have seen that Davidson attempts to avoid it, and Peacocke to espouse it, though they both regard themselves as non-reductionists. What I hope to prove is that there is not a great difference between translation or analytical reductionism on the one hand and the 'nothing-but' approach on the other. One reason why the difference is less than some philosophers imply is that not all analytic or translation reductionism involves the translation of mental descriptions into explicit and specific physical descriptions. Analytical behaviourism and Carnapian physicalism required this, but it is the whole point of topic-neutral analysis and translation that such topic-neutral analysis does not: and this is the form of translation favoured by contemporary analytical reductionists. In the following section I shall show, first, how 'nothing-but' materialism avoids the forms of strong reductionism that Davidson and others explicitly mention, and, second, that is does not avoid but requires the topic-neutral reductionism they seem conveniently to ignore.

4 TRANSLATION AND TOPIC NEUTRALITY
It seems very likely that it is impossible to match descriptions in terms of nations with descriptions of the behaviour of individuals. I do not see, for example, what finite or recursive account of the behaviour of individuals would be co-extensive with the predicate 'is going to war'. There are an indefinite number of ways that people might make war. Therefore there can be no translation of such expressions into ones which range over individuals. This is, of course, quite compatible with the fact that any particular instance of war-making is just the activity of individuals. The absence of type–type identities between objects on the different levels of

description does not prevent there being token–token identities. There is nothing special about the relation between nations and individuals in this respect. It applies in general to the relations between whole and part — at least if the wholes in question are not natural kinds. For example, one cannot define what it is to be a table in terms of atomic structure, for the variety of actual and possible configurations of actual and possible types of stuff which could provide a surface suitable for dining off is indefinite. Similarly, there will be no extensional equivalence between being a table and having a given arrangement of a given type of microscopic part; for neither nations nor tables is there a straightforward translation reduction of the Carnapian or analytical behaviourist sort. This does not, however, mean that there are no logical relations between these different levels of discourse. Call the two levels 'L_1' and 'L_2', L_1 being that which refers to the more atomic entities. For any statements in L_2 there will be statements in L_1 which entail them: if the statements in L_2 are true, the corresponding statements in L_1 will be true; but though statements in L_2 are entailed by statements in L_1, statements in L_2 do not entail particular statements in L_1. Thus it will always be possible to give sufficient conditions for the truth of L_2 statements in L_1 terms, though never to give necessary conditions. On reflexion this is obvious, for it is only a slightly more formal way of saying that, for example, though we cannot say that any particular series of individual human actions is necessary to every war, we can describe a series of events which indubitably counts as — that is, is sufficient for — there being a war. Similarly, though we cannot say that any particular atomic theory or structure is entailed by the existence of tables, the existence of certain sorts of atoms in certain structures entails the existence of tables.

The fact that L_1 statements are not necessary for the truth of L_2 statements means they are not equivalent and therefore not inter-translatable. But the fact that certain L_1 statements are sufficient for the truth of L_2 statements means that L_2 statements can be analysed in 'L_1 compatible' terms. That is, they must have an analysis which is consistent with their truth being entailed by the truth of L_1 statements. In other words, statements about entities in the ontology of L_2 must be analysable in a way that is *topic-neutral* about whether these objects are in fact nothing but the entities in the ontology of L_1. If there is not this openness or neutrality it could not turn out that L_1 statements were true and logically sufficient for true L_2 statements, or that L_2 entities were nothing but arrangements of L_1 entities.

The conclusion we are reaching, therefore, is that where there is ontological reduction of the 'nothing-but' sort, there is also analytical reduction of the topic-neutral, though not explicit, variety. Assuming that it is part of our common-sense concept of a table that tables are not made of smaller parts which are themselves tables, one could analyse 'table' as 'Whatever arrangement or structure of parts artificially put together constitutes a flat, raised surface suitable for eating off, writing at etc.' This would be a topic-neutral account of tables — neutral, that is, about what the real essence of any particular table might be. Such topic-neutral definitions have more point when the definiendum is a natural kind — for example, 'Water is whatever structure underlies the transparent liquid drunk by humans and which falls as rain'. It has more point in these cases because we expect there to be one only or a systematic range of structures which meet such a definition in the case of a natural kind, and therefore it is more likely to be useful to think of these macroscopic objects in terms of their micro-structures than it will for artifacts which are structurally more random. Given the possibility of such topic-neutral definitions, there will be some micro-level L_1 descriptions from which it follows that what is present is a table, or water, etc.

5 THE 'HOLISM OF THE MENTAL'

The doctrine of the *holism of the mental* (yet again a doctrine associated with the name of Donald Davidson) may be employed at this point to draw a red herring across the track of our argument (Davidson, 1971: 92). It may be argued that no description of any physical states or bodily motions is sufficient for the satisfaction of any particular mental descriptions because there are always an indefinite number of ways in which the behaviour of human bodies can be interpreted. Thus some behaviour that might be taken as exhibiting a belief that p with a desire that q could equally well (though perhaps less naturally) be interpreted as exhibiting a belief that r and a desire that s. It is not clear that this degree of slack in interpretation is unique to the relation of physical and psychological states. Perhaps the conduct of large groups of people massacring each other could be interpreted as a rain-making ritual of a bizarre sort. An example of this sort of thing is found in the old chestnut about the foreign visitor to England who went to watch his first cricket match. On returning home he reported in wonder the details of what he had taken to be a rain-making ceremony of astounding efficacy. It is not clear that vagueness of this sort differs in kind from the way in which evidence always under-determines theory, leaving the possibility of more than one theory. Nor is it obvious that there are not canons of good, sensible and simple interpretation in the case of psychology parallel in principle to those in more rigorous sciences. Letting these matters lie, all that the holistic objection shows is (a) that, if one is in the business of making psychological interpretations at all, then certain physical descriptions will be sufficient to show that some psychological ascription is appropriate; and (b) that the physical descriptions, together with certain canons of interpretation, will be sufficient for some definite psychological ascriptions. This latter condition does not rule out a vagueness giving rise to difficult cases where one does not know what states to ascribe: there are structures of which it is not clear whether they are to be counted as tables, but this does not affect the reducibility of tables. In all cases certain canons of interpretation are required, but they are always implicit in our practice — this is shown by the fact that we agree broadly on what states of mind to ascribe to people, and on what forms of individual behaviour to count as making war, etc. In the case of micro-to-macro descriptions where the microscopic descriptions belong in a special science, perhaps the canons of interpretation will take the form of bridging laws connecting types of microscopic structure to types of macroscopic property (e. g. that clouds of atoms of a certain sort guarantee solidity; others, malleability, etc.).

6 RÉSUMÉ

The situation can be summed up as follows. It seems to be agreed that if predicates and states of class M supervene on predicates and states of class P, then at least the following two conditions hold: (1) M cannot vary independently of P; (2) M-language cannot be translated into P-language. The second condition rules out one explanation of the first; so we might reasonably be puzzled about the nature of the necessity that governs (1). One intention seems to be that it should be some form of *a posteriori* necessity akin to that which Kripke attaches to identity statements. This would be a necessity such that it needed to be discovered, but once it had been discovered then we could see that things could not be otherwise. But in discussing Peacocke's attempt to apply this principle here, we saw that it cannot be applied so as to make the occurrence of the appropriate P-states without

M-states impossible. We are, therefore, constrained to look for a type of *a priori* necessity compatible with the second condition. In fact the 'nation—individuals' example gives the model for such a relation, namely that P-statements entail M-statements, though not vice-versa.[2] However, as I have argued, this means that M-statements can be analysed in topic-neutral or 'P-compatible' terms. Whether one calls such analyses 'translations' might be a matter of taste, but certainly the M-statements and the corresponding neutral statements will be necessarily equivalent; otherwise we would not have an acceptable philosophical analysis. If this is correct then the super-venience relation does not give us a new way to an intuitively acceptable non-reductive form of materialism, but rather entails the modern sort of reductive or 'translation' materialism associated with such philosophers as J. J. C. Smart and D. M. Armstrong.

7 FUNCTIONALISM, REDUCTION AND TOPIC NEUTRALITY

These considerations help us to locate the popular theory known as 'functionalism'. Hilary Putnam (1975a) and others, such as Fodor (1976: 2-26) and Wilkes (1978: 66), regard their theory as non-reductive. Their ground for this claim is that, on their theory, psychological vocabulary is no more translatable into explicitly physicalist or behaviourist terms than a computer program is trans-latable into the language of computer hardware engineering. We have already seen that absence of translatability does not mean irreducibility; there are also other reservations to be made about the functionalist strategy. Most important, the analogy between psychological discourse and computer programs is imperfect in a central respect. The *significant* output of computers (though not, say, of robots) consists in 'utterances' in the language of their program. If we distinguish between linguistic behaviour and other forms of behaviour, the computer's significant behaviour is entirely linguis-tic. Its 'mental processes' terminate in 'sayings' not 'doings'. For this reason, there need be no essential correlations between its states as defined in terms of its program and its output conceived in terms of non-linguistic behaviour. In so far as language is interpreted in terms of its connexion with non-linguistic behaviour, a computer's lan-guage cannot be interpreted from the behaviour of the computer but

2 This strong interpretation of supervenience is found in Blackburn, 1971, and Kirk, 1979. They show that supervenience involves entailment but they do not make clear that this is *a priori* entailment rather than entailment which rests on *a posteriori* necessity. The latter point is required if we are to show that supervenience is merely a form of reduction.

from its connexion with the behaviour of humans. This is not meant to be a point about machines as such, for it need not apply to robots — that is, machines which act non-linguistically as well as linguistically — but only about machines without significant non-linguistic behaviour. The point is that it is the absence of such behaviour that isolates the programmatic from the physical level and seems to obviate the necessity for the interpretation of the former in terms of the latter. The significance of human (or robotic) mental states is, on the other hand, fairly directly connected with their influence on non-linguistic behaviour — actual movement around and manipulation of the physical environment. Putnam's comparison of psychological states with what he calls the 'logical' states of a computer can thus be seen to be misleading, if 'logical' is to be contrasted with 'behavioural' (1975a, 370 f). The significance of what a computer does is 'logical' in the sense of drawing its meaning only from its linguistic output as defined by the program. The functional states of men or robots are not in this sense 'logical' states. Even where the output is linguistic, that language presumably derives sense from its connexion with other forms of behaviour. This means that, in at least a relatively unsystematic way, the functional significance of our mental states does ultimately come out in behavioural terms: the divide is crossed, even though the mapping of the one onto the other is loose and open to a variety of interpretations. (My comments above concerning Davidson's holism are relevant here.) Therefore, though a functional state will not have a *simple* behavioural contribution, that it possesses such a contribution is what makes it functional.

The only way to understand functionalism is by comparison with the individual—nation and atom—table cases considered above. It takes psychological language as a way of interpreting at a certain 'molar' or macroscopic level the significance of behaviour and the significance of certain biochemical events in terms of the contribution they make to behaviour. It is, therefore, reductionist in just the way that nations are reducible to individuals and tables to atoms. Superficially, it might seem that functionalism is very different from these other cases, because there is no suggestion that the relation between function and embodiment is that of whole to part. However, a nation is not just a collection of individuals, but individuals working in a certain way: this is true even of atoms and tables: thus the element of function or mode of operation is present in the other

30

cases. The common point is that, given canons of interpretation, a sufficiently extensive physical description will entail a psychological one, for the psychological one supervenes on the physical behaviour of which it is an interpretation.

This means that functionalism is much closer to behaviourism than its protagonists seem inclined to pretend. Thus, although no exact behavioural analysis need — or can — be given of what it is to think or feel in general, or think p or feel f in particular; nevertheless, the functionalist must believe that particular cases of a person's thinking or feeling are no more than his possessing a certain behavioural readiness. This does mean that some general behaviouristic account of thinking, feeling etc. is required. That is, it would have to be possible to explain what sort of functioning is appropriate to each type of psychological state and why that counts as appropriate. A general account of what makes it appropriate to deem a certain functional state — that is, a physically embodied behavioural disposition — to be a believing, a feeling etc. must in principle be available; otherwise there would be no rationale to our so interpreting them.

I have made no mention of a feature of functionalism of which functionalists themselves make much. They insist that the function of a mental state may include the production of *further mental states* instead of behaviour (e.g. Block, 1978: 262) Have I, by ignoring this fact, made it seem easier to assimilate functionalism to behaviourism than it really is? The answer to this question is implicit in what has gone before. A normal computer program draws its sense from a context which does not essentially involve computers. Its subject matter will usually be mathematical, or otherwise related to that subject, problems in which the program is designed to solve. The computer language is in that way independent of the computer. When humans employ psychological discourse they talk about themselves and each other. If a certain psychological state is interpreted in terms of its function in producing some form of behaviour, then its significance is, in principle, plain. If it is interpreted in terms of the function of producing a further mental state, then we await elucidation of the function of that before the significance of the first can be made plain or 'cashed'. It can only be at the level of, or by reference to, behaviour, that these functional states declare their colours. Once we are aware of the behavioural—functional significance of some type of mental state M, we can intelligibly think of

31

another type of mental state N having the function, in some contexts, of producing M. But only as it comes out in behaviour will any of it be interpreted. This would not be so if we believed in old-fashioned mental contents, but as these have been abolished and as we are not supposed to be talking about states of the hardware, then nothing not itself a further function apart from actual behaviour remains for the cashing of these states.[3]

Functionalists like Putnam have tended to be shy about dealing with sensations and consciousness; they are happier with intellectual states such as belief. But when Wilkes, in the course of a thorough working out of the theory, comes to deal with sensations and consciousness she takes the most radically reductive line of all and denies that such things exist: she chooses, that is, the disappearance theory of sensations and says that consciousness is a concept unknown to the Greeks and foisted on modern philosophy by Descartes (1978: 101ff). Wilkes is not being eccentric in developing the theory in this way, for if functionalism is to provide a complete account of mind and not leave 'raw feels' untouched it must either treat them in a behaviouristic way or deny their existence: as far as satisfying intuition is concerned, there is little difference between these approaches.[4]

There is one feature of other reductive theories that functionalism is supposed to avoid, namely the need to give a topic-neutral account of our knowledge of and reference to mental states. However, the parallel with other supervenience theories extends to this matter. The meaning of a computer program, it might be argued, does not require to be given a topic-neutral analysis. The comparison between mental states and the contents of programs is however, misleading. In a program which instructs a machine 'Add two and two', it is not the embedded content 'two and two' which requires a functional or topic-neutral treatment, but the notion of adding. The computer's adding is a genuine event in the physical world. As such it is a functional event supervening on — by being enmattered or realised in — the workings of the computer hardware. That it is so

---

3   That it is regressive and ultimately vicious to define functions or powers in terms of other functions or powers is shown in ch. 7.4, in the discussion of modern conceptions of matter.

4   In ch. 5 we shall see how the disappearance theory requires functionalism: the two are naturally wedded. We have already noticed the close connexion between functionalism and behaviourism: the latter in its most primitive form involved the denial of the existence of consciousness and was therefore a form of disappearance theory. It is neither too fanciful nor unfair to regard the fashionable functionalism-with-disappearance as a return to the most primitive forms of behaviourism as far as its treatment of consciousness is concerned. See Searle, 1981, for some further persuasive arguments to the conclusion that functionalism does not differ in crucial respects from behaviourism.

realised is part of what is involved in giving a functional analysis of this activity, for it has to be the functioning *of something* which realises the program. Therefore we can present as a paraphrase of 'The machine is adding two and two', 'Something is going on in that machine which realises the operation of adding two and two.' The latter paraphrase is philosophically illuminating because it exposes the fact that in referring to a computer adding, one is referring to some process the exact nature of which one may not know, but which realises the adding. This paraphrase makes it plain that a sentence referring to a computer's adding involves referring to or hypothesising some process in the hardware. The *meaning* of the term 'add' needs no analysis because it has a plain sense defined in other, purely mathematical, contexts. Therefore we have a topic-neutral element in the reference of the expression but not in the sense. The situation is different with psychological vocabulary. 'Think', 'perceive', 'feel' etc. have their sense from the psychological case; the functionalist analysis of mind therefore enters more deeply into our interpretation of them than our functionalist interpretation of computers enters into the vocabulary of programs. It is only a first move to point out the topic-neutral element in their reference. In the same way as for the computer, '*S* believes that *p*' can be paraphrased thus: 'There is something going on in *S* which realises believing that *p*.' But, for reasons given above, mental states are functional–behavioural, not merely logical. They get their sense from their role as part of a holistic interpretation of behaviour. Consequently some general behavioural analysis of 'believes' must, in principle, be added to the topic-neutral mode of reference. Put together these will give something of the general form: 'Something is going on in *S* which tends to cause belief-that-*p* behaviour'. We must assume that that behaviour could, if necessary, be spelled out or at least illustrated, for otherwise it would not be recognisable and we could not make the ascription. The paraphrase we have arrived at is of the form of those paraphrases provided by the causal analysis of mind; a topic-neutral account of the sense of psychological language.

Daniel Dennett propounds a theory which he calls 'intentionalism' and which he claims is one stage less reductionist than other forms of functionalism (1979: xix). The arguments employed above tell just as strongly against his version of the theory. Other functionalists, he says, analyse cognitive states as the realisation of some logical state of a Turing machine (ibid.: xvi). For example,

(x) $(x$ believes that snow is white$\equiv x$ 'realises' some Turing machine k in logical state a).

He, by contrast, is satisfied with

(x) $(x$ believes that snow is white$\equiv x$ can be predicatively attributed the belief that snow is white).

Against the accusation that this latter schema is blatently circular, he replies: 'All we need to make an informative answer of this formula is a systematic way of making the attributions alluded to on the right-hand side' (ibid.: xvii). He argues that because the 'logical state' analysis does not require further reduction in more explicitly physicalist terms, then neither does his mentalist analysis. But I have already explained why psychological-cum-behavioural states need analysis while properly logical states of a computer do not. Dennett's comparison is misconceived and so, therefore, is his easy way round reductionism. His claim to believe that reduction is a mistaken goal for the physicalist (ibid.) looks less than convincing when one looks at the details of his own system. Not only does he espouse eliminative materialism for those Cartesian entities he dislikes (ibid.: xx), he also falls surreptitiously into topic-neutral paraphrase when convenient (see chapter 5.2 for an explanation of why eliminative materialists are bound to take this further step). On concluding his physicalist account of pain he says:

I recommend ... giving up all 'essential' features of pain and letting pain states be whatever 'natural kind' states the brain scientists find (if they do find any) that normally produce all the normal effects. (ibid.: 228)

The formula 'A pain is whatever state normally produces pain-behaviour' presents a standard topic-neutral analysis of pain.

That functionalism is nothing other than a version of the causal theory will be confirmed in chapter 4, where we shall find that neither is more adequate than behaviourism.

34

3

Behaviourism and stimulus materialism

I BEHAVIOURISM, DISPOSITIONS AND PHYSICALISM

The failure of non-reductive forms of materialism leads us to consider reductive theories. The most popular contemporary versions of reductive materialism, namely the central state theories of Smart and Armstrong, were developed in response to the inadequacies of behaviourism. They also retained important behaviouristic components. So it is natural to begin our discussion by plotting the logical paths which have led from behaviourism to central state materialism.

According to the most naive formulation of behaviourism, to be in a certain mental state is to be behaving in some supposedly appropriate way. Thus, to be in pain is to be pain-behaving. The inadequacies of such a naive approach were always apparent: overt behaviour is neither necessary nor sufficient for possession of the mental state. Some people can suffer pain and repress the normal behavioural response; others – for example actors – might exhibit the behaviour when they lack the pain. Behaviourists have tended to adopt either of two possible modifications to the theory to meet this problem. We shall see that both responses point towards central state materialism. The first modification, and the more popular one among philosophers, is to identify a mental state with the disposition towards behaviour, rather than with the behaviour itself. The first problem with this theory is to explain what one means by 'disposition'. Ryle (1949) popularised this general approach to the philosophy of mind and he interpreted 'disposition' in a non-realist (sometimes called 'phenomenalist') sense. For Ryle, to say that s has a disposition to $\emptyset$ is to say that he has $\emptyset$d, is $\emptyset$ing, will $\emptyset$ or would $\emptyset$ in certain specified appropriate circumstances. According to this theory, a disposition neither is, nor essentially involves, any causal state underlying the potential behaviour.

While it is no doubt true of someone in pain and suppressing pain-behaviour that he would manifest that behaviour in some 'appropriate' circumstances, this fact does not distinguish him from other sensitive creatures. Someone *not* now in pain *would* manifest pain-behaviour under appropriate circumstances − for example, if struck a sharp blow on the shins. The account presented defines the capacity to feel pain, but not the sensation of pain. This is hardly surprising, for the former is uncontroversially a dispositional notion whilst the latter is not. Ryle himself did not try to apply his analysis to occurrent events such as sensations, reserving it for moods, emotions and traits of character, for which it is more suitable. In order to pick out the situation where the subject actually feels the pain one can make reference to the occurrent events or stimuli that actually cause pain. Thus one would say that someone is in pain if both (1) he has been subject to the sort of stimulus that normally causes pain-behaviour and (2) he is disposed to that behaviour. Condition (1) does indicate the conditions under which someone might be expected to feel pain but, like (2), it is neither necessary nor sufficient. It is not necessary because someone who has not been subject to any of the normal external pain-stimuli might feel pain: only the internal activity of the pain centres in the brain are fully necessary. It is not sufficient because anaesthetic or neurological peculiarity can lead someone to fail to feel pain when subjected to normally painful stimuli. In order to make (1) adequate one has to abandon the original behaviourist notion of a stimulus as something external affecting the organism, for only the activity of the relevant portion of the central nervous system itself will be causally both necessary and sufficient. Thus we can say that someone is in pain (1') if and only if there is that sort of activity in the central nervous system typically associated with the sort of external stimuli which damage the organism and (2') this central activity causes or disposes him to pain-behaviour. Condition (2') involves a modification of our concept of disposition: it is now represented as essentially involving an internal cause. This is the realist theory of dispositions, adopted, for example, by Armstrong (1968: 85-8). Different forms of physicalism emphasise one of these conditions at the expense of the other. Smart (1963) and Levin (1979), who propound what I shall call 'stimulus materialism', emphasise the former: Armstrong (1968) and Lewis (1966), with their causal analysis of mind, emphasise the latter. In order to derive the physicalist theories that emerge from (1') and (2') one must eliminate the explicit reference to activities of the central nervous system, for no such reference is present in our lay psychological discourse. However, according to Smart and Armstrong, we were always aware that mental states involved *something or other internal* playing the appropriate role, although we knew not what, nor even whether it was physical. This *topic-neutral* aspect of our knowledge is explained more fully in section 4 below. When applied to the two versions of physicalism mentioned above we get the formulae:

(i) s is disposed to pain-behave if and only if s has active in him that which is normally active in him when he is subjected to paradigms of pain stimuli.

(ii) s is disposed to pain-behave if and only if s has active in him that which has a causal tendency to produce pain-behaviour.

These propositions correspond almost exactly to the doctrines of Smart and Armstrong. It is noteworthy that (ii) can be seen as a version of the behaviourist theory that mental states are identical with dispositions to behaviour combined with a realist theory of dispositions; for in that case to say that one has a disposition to do something will be to say that there is some state within one tending to cause one to do that thing. Armstrong acknowledges that this disagreement about dispositions is at the heart of the difference between his theory and standard forms of behaviourism (1968: 88).

2 COVERT BEHAVIOUR AND PHYSICALISM

We must now return almost to the beginning. We reacted to the inadequacies of naive behaviourism − that is, to the fact that not all mental states are accompanied by behaviour − by invoking the notion of a disposition to behave. Some behaviourists, however, took another road and it will be instructive to see how that also leads to physicalism. The alternative road is to deny that mental states are ever present in the absence of behaviour: they are sometimes present in the absence of *overt* behaviour, but then there will be *covert* behaviour. Thus if someone fails to show his pain overtly, nevertheless there will be an internal reaction of some sort − for example, a tensing of muscles or rising blood pressure − as he steels himself against the pain. In these cases this covert behaviour will be what constitutes being in pain. Therefore naive behaviourism stands, though with this extended sense to 'behaviour'.

This suggestion falls to the same difficulty as the suggestion that an external stimulus was a necessary condition for pain, namely that the only internal or covert activity that is essential to pain, on any materialist theory, is that activity of the central nervous system which is a necessary and sufficient causal condition for it. Therefore, a man who is totally paralysed, such that only the pain centres of his brain react and none of his muscles can tense or his heart alter its beat, will still be in pain when those centres are appropriately active. Thus the only essential behaviour will be activity that is not under the agent's direct control; it is not in the ordinary sense something that he *does* at all. 'Behaviour' now covers any form of bodily activity, whether or not it falls within the control or consciousness of the subject.

We are now back to the problem of how to pick out the relevant processes in the central nervous system and again the Smart and Armstrong analyses present themselves. There is nothing novel about the discovery that behaviourism collapses into physicalism in attempting to extend the concept of covert behaviour to cover all secret mental states. Broad exposed this line of retreat:

When the Behaviourist says that all mental processes reduce without residue to the fact that the body is behaving in a certain specific way he does not mean to confine himself to gross overt actions like shrieking or kicking ... He always includes at least such bodily movements as changes of blood-pressure, incipient movements in the tongue and throat ... and so on ...
But it is very difficult to get the Behaviourist to stop at this point. When overt behaviour, supplemented by changes of blood-pressure, incipient movements of the throat, etc., seems inadequate to make the behaviouristic analysis plausible, the Behaviourist is very liable to appeal to hypothetical, molecular movements in the brain and nervous system. If you say to him that two obviously different mental processes, A and B are accompanied by indistinguishable molar behaviour, or that qualitatively indistinguishable mental processes are accompanied on different occasions by obviously different kinds of molar behaviour, he is liable to say: 'Well, at any rate, the correlated molecular changes in the brain and nervous system must have been different in the one case and exactly alike in the other.' ... The Behaviourist then proceeds to *identify* the mental processes with the supposed molecular changes ... In this form of course there is nothing new about Behaviourism; it is just old-fashioned materialism which has crossed the Atlantic under an *alias*. (1925: 616-17)

We have seen that behaviourism moves naturally to physicalism as it tries to meet various defects. There is another side to this coin, namely that many forms of physicalism are less radically different from behaviourism than their protagonists would have us think. We have already seen this in the case of functionalism, and in chapter 4.6

in the discussion of Armstrong's theory of introspection we shall see that it is true of the causal theory.

3 BEHAVIOUR, INTROSPECTION AND PHYSICALISM

This discussion of behaviourism is intended primarily as an introduction to and explanation of the derivation of modern forms of physicalism. I have, therefore, said nothing so far about the most common objection to behaviourism, namely that it is so counterintuitive as to be manifestly false because it is not true to the data of consciousness. Anyone who has had a pain knows that it does not consist simply in tendencies to bodily movement; anyone who thinks or perceives without reacting knows that his current activity does not simply consist in the fact that he will or would do something or be internally caused to do something at some other time. These intuitive objections are objections against the form of behaviourism that invokes dispositions. Those who prefer the alternative strategy of relying on covert behaviour have the beginnings of an answer to this intuitive objection to behaviourism. They can say that what one is aware of when one is conscious of thought, perception or pain which is not manifesting itself overtly is the covert behaviour. This form of behaviourism avoids the objections that Armstrong brings, for he assumes that the behaviourist resorts to the dispositional analysis.

Farrell is among those who invoke covert behaviour to explain the experiencing of mental acts. Asking what it is that a behaviourist can notice and time, when introspecting his own perception, he says, 'When x times himself here, say by stopping a stop watch, all that he can time is his "seeing" – e.g. his subvocal "Ah! that's it", his accompanying release of breath and muscular tension and so forth' (1950: 178). There are various objections to this approach. We have already considered general objections to the notion of covert behaviour. Additionally, Farrell seems oblivious to the difficulty of saying what, for a behaviourist, sub-vocal speech (i.e. speech without physical sound) is – auditory mental images do not enter his ontology – and overlooks the problem of what *noticing* the muscle tensing comes to. We saw in chapter 1 that the materialist is not helped by making physical, as against phenomenal, objects the objects of awareness as long as the notion of awareness itself remains unreduced. Farrell is not, therefore, helped simply by making muscle tensions the objects of perception instead of visual sense-data.

However, he is beginning to develop a line of thought which physicalists will take up. Self-consciousness, they will say (as we shall see) consists in the monitoring of internal processes. These processes will be central and not peripheral, unlike muscle tensings, in accordance with our previous conclusions. We have also seen that once the covert behaviour becomes central it becomes indistinguishable from the realist base for the disposition postulated by the supposedly alternative analysis. Therefore, the dispositional and covert behaviour forms of behaviourism are brought together in their accounts of consciousness by invoking the notion of the monitoring of central forms of covert activity, which are the typical products of appropriate external stimuli and which constitute the dispositions to act overtly. This account of consciousness we shall discuss in considerable detail in chapter 4.

The conclusion then is that all roads lead from behaviourism to physicalism. But whereas pursuit of the dispositional theory leads to the causal theory, or functionalism (ignoring for the moment Smart's stimulus theory), pursuit of the covert behaviour theory leads to that doctrine of consciousness which the causal theorists will claim gives their theory such great advantages over behaviourism. Without this latter component these forms of physicalism are no more than behaviourism with dispositions construed realistically. We shall see later that real weaknesses reside in the use causal theorists need to make of a doctrine of consciousness as internal perception.

4 SMART AND TOPIC NEUTRALITY

Stimulus materialism, roughly as expressed above, was the first form of central state materialism to be developed from behaviourism. We shall find that the stimulus theory is a blind alley and that it must, logically, give way to the causal approach. This was in fact the historical progression. However, it is necessary to investigate the stimulus approach, partly because it has recently been vigorously defended at length, and partly because discussion of it will expose a fatal flaw common to all forms of topic-neutral reductive materialism.

The classic statement of the stimulus theory is given by J. J. C. Smart:

The man who reports a yellowish orange after-image does so in effect as follows: *'What is going on in me is like what is going on in me when* my eyes are

40

open, the light is normal etc. etc. and there really is a yellowish-orange patch on the wall.' In this sentence the word 'like' is meant to be used in such a way that something can be like itself... With this sense of 'like' the above formula will do for a report that one is having a veridical sense datum too. Notice that the italicised words *'what is going on in me is like what is going on in me when ...'* are topic neutral. (1963: 94-5)

Smart was responsible for introducing the concept of topic neutrality into the discussion of materialism, and the idea has been very widely taken up. The term has already been used in an earlier chapter of this essay. A brief account of this notion will, therefore, be relevant to what follows, especially to the discussion of the causal theory.

The object in introducing the concept of topic neutrality is to provide a reductive paraphrase of mentalistic idiom in a way which eliminates specifically mental predicates. The intention is to provide some analysis of mental ascriptions which leaves a possibility that the possession of certain physical properties should be logically sufficient for the truth of such ascriptions. In order to achieve this, Smart claims that the mentalistic idiom is topic neutral; that is, it specifies a condition of a person in a way which is open enough to leave it logically possible that something physical or something non-physical should make the ascription true. Such a paraphrase would have to specify, in a plausible way, what it is that makes a state a mental state; this specification would have to be given in terms which might apply to an object solely in virtue of its physical features.

In general, for a statement to be topic neutral is for it to pick out some individual or type of individual without ascribing any intrinsic properties to the thing that it picks out: for an object to be known topic neutrally would thus be for it to be known under such a description, or (in those cases where neutrality is most interesting) for it to be known under such a description and no other non-neutral (i.e. intrinsic) description. Perhaps this characterisation could be weakened somewhat: we might say that knowledge of something was significantly neutral if our knowledge of it was neutral with respect to some important intrinsic features − that is, if some important aspect of it was known only neutrally. Perhaps, that is, neutrality might be taken as relative to certain particular alternatives and concerns and not as regarding all features. There are, without doubt, many instances of topic-neutral statements and topic-neutral knowledge. For example, an object is described or known neutrally when it is described or known under some power-ascribing description; for example, 'that which causes cancer', or when it is picked out as the object of some act, 'whoever it was that was kicked'. The former type of case, well known in natural science, is probably the most common instance of types of object, in other ways unknown, being referred to topic neutrally. The causal theory of mind follows this pattern of analysis. In most cases the description will not be wholly neutral concerning the type of object that is thought to fill the bill; the context, at least, will show that some generic type of thing is in mind. Thus, when one refers to 'the cause of cancer, whatever it is', generally one will assume that one is referring to something physical which falls into one of the categories of type of thing known to cause illness: or, when Smart instances 'Somebody is coming through the garden' as a topic-neutral reference, he does not wish to deny that the sentence implies that the thing coming through the garden is a human being. When the technique is applied to mental states, however, the neutrality involved is of a very radical sort, for the whole purpose of the exercise is to allow that the mental might fall either into the category of physical substance or into some other category.

5 THE MAIN WEAKNESS IN STIMULUS MATERIALISM

The basic weakness of the stimulus theory and the cause of its replacement by the causal approach is that it has no plausible account of what makes an internal state constitute an experience. The answer apparently intended is that an internal state counts as an experience of x if it was brought about by x as its stimulus. The inadequacy of this is patent, for external objects wreak many changes within our body without our experiencing either the internal changes or their cause. Someone who cannot feel pain is internally affected when he puts his hand on to the hot-plate, but he does not experience anything. It is simply wrong to equate all internal effects of stimuli with experiences. Nor will it help to say that it must be an internal change of a sort *typically* caused by that sort of stimulus. It is true that, on one interpretation of 'typically', this rules out the abnormal inability to feel pain; but, typically, radiation causes internal changes, though we do not perceive it. It would, of course, be possible to stipulate that the only changes that counted were in certain areas of the central nervous system — namely those areas which are in fact associated with experience – but that would not explain why the events in those regions counted as experiences (as against merely causing them). It is obvious enough what seems to be missing. If we are to operate within a reductionist framework, what is missing in the cases of the analgesiac and the normal man bombarded by radiation is any immediate disposition to respond: there is nothing tending to cause them to behave as if they experienced the stimulus.

6 EXPERIENCE AND STIMULUS MATERIALISM

The stimulus theory is principally associated with Smart, but it has more recently been defended at length in a modified version by Michael Levin. Neither of them takes the path outlined above of shifting the emphasis from stimulus to response. The methods they adopt share a very general similarity. Roughly speaking, they both say or imply that the internal states which count as experiences are those of which we are aware. Smart talks of *reporting similarities* between brain states, and Levin of *intuiting their essences*. Let us consider Smart's approach first. When explaining how we can recognise experiences without our building sensible qualities into them as their internal objects, he argues as follows:

> For this account to be successful, it is necessary that we should be able to report two processes as like one another without being able to say in what respect they are alike. An experience of having an after-image may be classified as like the experience I have when I see an orange, and this likeness, on my view, must consist in a neurophysiological pattern. But of course we are not aware of the pattern; at most we are able to report the similarity. (1963: 95)

Talk of reporting and classifying similarities implies recognising them. If Smart is not to fall back into the mentalism his theory is designed to avoid, this recognition must be construed behaviourally, in terms of dispositions to verbal and other discriminatory behaviour. This, no doubt, explains why he does not talk of *recognising* or *being aware* of similarities, but of *reporting* and *classifying* them. But by so doing Smart has altered the emphasis of his theory. What makes an internal state an experience is now not simply that it has a certain cause, but that it itself prompts or causes in us a certain discriminatory response. On Smart's theory, the response is directed towards the internal state, not towards the original stimulus, for it is the similarities between the internal states that are being recognised. This gives a version of the causal theory of mind, though one

43

differing from Armstrong's in that it involves a representative theory of perception. A causal theorist would explain *seeing a yellow after-image* in some such manner as the following:

There is something going on in me which is apt to produce discriminatory behaviour of the sort I am normally disposed to in the presence of a yellow object.

Smart's theory is now very similar to this; it could be paraphrased as:

There is something going on in me which is apt to produce discriminatory behaviour with regard to itself (i.e. with regard to the internal state) and this behaviour is of a sort to which I am normally disposed when what is going on in me is caused by a yellow object.

The only difference between these two formulae is that in the latter case the object of my causally grounded disposition is the internal state caused by the stimulus, whereas in the former case it is the stimulus itself. One might think that, other things being equal, one ought to prefer a direct realist theory to a representative one. This might seem particularly so when choosing between such reductive theories, for it is very obscure in what way the appropriate behaviour could be said to have the internal state, as opposed to the yellow thing, as its object, for the behaviour will apparently be with regard to some external yellow thing. However, Smart has to make the internal state the object of the disposition if he is to retain the idea that it is similarities between things 'going on in me' that I am recognising. We shall see in the next chapter that Armstrong's doctrine of consciousness as perception of our own brains somewhat erodes the difference between his position and Smart's; but what is significant for our present discussion is that Smart has been forced to shift his emphasis from the stimulus as what individuates the experience to its response-producing role.

7 LEVIN'S THEORY

Levin's theory is stranger than Smart's. Levin says that we 'intuit the essence' of our experiences (1979: 120). As experiences are supposed to be brain states and as we gain no explicit knowledge about our brains simply by being conscious of our experiences, this seems a strange expression. Levin admits that 'the only facts [the subject] knows about pains are circumstantial' (1979: 119). There are two very odd features of this account. First, it employs the notion of an intuition which is cognitively vacuous. We are supposed to intuit the essences of our experiences without coming to know anything about their intrinsic nature. This is surely a bizarre use of 'intuition', or 'essence', or both. Second, the concept of intuiting is hardly a physicalistic one. It is not the sort of notion one would expect to be employed without explanation by a philosopher who regards himself as a topic-neutral reductionist in a Smartian tradition. It may be that Levin would give a reductive – presumably behaviouristic – analysis of such intuitions. If so then a cognitively neutral 'intuiting the essence' of experiences would not materially differ from recognising their similarities. But I do not think that Levin intends this, for he helps himself to other cognate notions. When discussing after-images he simply says that having an after-image is like seeing, and appears to feel no need to give a reductive account of what it is to see. In a long book he makes no attempt to give a materialist analysis of perception as such. All he says about genuine perception is that it is a 'direct conscious encounter' and that it is 'a brain state, in some causal relation' to the appropriate physical thing (1979: 107). Which is to say that he thinks he can help himself to the notion of direct experience, with the gloss that it is, in some way, a causal concept. The reason why he believes that such a blatantly mentalistic idiom as 'direct awareness' is available to him is that he thinks that the objects and therefore the experiential content of such acts are unproblematically physical: ' "Yellow" appears in [normal perceptual reports] because what is going on [in such cases] goes on when a yellow object is seen. There is no need to postulate a yellow interior object of awareness or a phenomenal yellowness to explain the "yellow" in [such reports]' (1979: 106). He also says that because illusions such as after-images are just 'like' perception, then '[the] yellow thing involved in having a yellow after-image is the lemon' (ibid.).

Putting together these two quotations we derive the following doctrines. The rationale of the first quotation is that the notion of *seeing* is entirely unproblematical – presumably because it is a 'direct awareness' of something external: because seeing is such a direct awareness it needs no internal object. The argument of the second quotation is that, as imaging is merely a recollecting of the purely physical object of perceiving, it no more stands in need of an internal object than does perception.

Levin presents himself as a reductionist. In fact he stands four-square with those philosophers we dismissed in chapter 1 for making

45

the elementary mistake of thinking that all that materialism required was that we avoid reifying sense contents. We showed there that the direct realist's notion of awareness is for the materialist just as unacceptable, in an unanalysed form, as are sense contents. Furthermore, even if perception could be explained in terms of an unproblematic awareness relation we could still not treat after-images as does Levin. The fact that such an image is the representation of what was originally present physically does not analyse or explain the present content of experience, for in having an after-image I am no longer directly aware of something physical.

It is because Levin does not recognise that such notions as 'awareness' or 'perception' are mentalistic, even if treated as relations without internal objects, and therefore does not see the need to give a reductive analysis of them, that he thinks he can help himself to the kin notion of intuition to explain our grasp of subjective experience. His statement that, contrasted with the causal theory, 'Smart's earlier account [of topic neutralism] is closer to the truth, and its simplicity makes it convenient to use' (1979: 118) could not be more wrong. Until it develops into the causal theory, as it does surreptitiously in Smart's own writing, it fails to be an account of experience at all. That Levin is impressed by its 'simplicity' shows only that he, more than Smart, has failed to grasp the nature of the problem.

8 TOPIC NEUTRALITY AND THE REALIST THEORY OF UNIVERSALS

As we have seen, Smart claims that we do not know the actual or intrinsic nature of our experiences: we know about them only topic neutrally as *whatever* internal state has a certain cause. But the fact that our knowledge of the nature of experience is topic neutral has serious consequences for our knowledge of the objects of our experience. *Ex hypothesi* the experience of having a yellow after-image is similar to that of seeing a yellow object in the relevant ways. Hallucinating something yellow could be exactly like seeing something yellow. Experiences are characterised by their objects. The afterimages or hallucinations referred to above are characterised by being *of something yellow*. If we gather nothing non-neutral about the nature of our experiences from self-consciousness or introspection then, presumably, experience presents its objects in this topic-neutral form. Smart might respond that his theory is not meant as an account of the objects of experience but only of the experiential *having* of those objects. This reply, however, entirely fails in its purpose.

Taking those cases where the object is definitely subjective or internal, such as after-images or hallucinations, the topic-neutral analysis must include them, or it is not a complete account of the subjective introspectable element in experience. We have already argued, in chapter 1.2, that the intentionality of these objects cannot validly be used as a reason for ignoring them. Whether one treats the objects of such experiences intentionally, extensionally or adverbially, *being-of-something-yellow* will remain an introspectable feature of those experiences. Smart in fact recognises this difficulty, at least by implication. His treatment of after-images in terms of the report 'What is going on in me is like what goes on when ...' shows that he does not think a materialist could allow unanalysed the report 'I see yellowly' or 'I have an experience-of-something-yellow'. It is in fact part of this materialist programme to analyse out reference to internal or intentional objects on the grounds that they are mentalistic entities. But if the adverbial or intentional aspects of experience are included within the range of our topic-neutral understanding then serious damage is done to our grasp of the nature of the objects of our experience and therefore to our grasp of the physical world we experience. If there is nothing grasped non-neutrally in experience, then the nature of yellow is caught only neutrally. But, experientially, after-images or (more likely) hallucinations are not thought of as essentially different from veridical experiences. Therefore, yellow is grasped only neutrally in normal experience. Nor is this just a feature of secondary qualities as objects of experience: if it were, some philosophers would be unmoved, for they regard secondary qualities as neutral, 'gappy' or unreal (e.g. Armstrong, 1968: 274f). It applies equally and in the same way to shape or movement when they are presented as internal objects of experience.

Smart's way of preventing topic-neutral knowledge from being simple ignorance is to argue that, though we know nothing about the intrinsic nature of experience, we can recognise similarity and dissimilarity relations between experiences. The same strategy would appear to be the only way available of treating our recognition of the neutrally presented internal objects of experience. Thus the only things we grasp about the nature of the objects of our experience from experience are their relations of similarity to and dissimilarity from each other, and we are forced to adopt a 'resemblance theory' account of qualities or universals as they are presented in experience.

I cannot here become embroiled in a discussion of the theory of universals: that would require an essay of its own. What I can try to do is to show that this resemblance account of the internal objects of experience is barely compatible with a realist theory of universals: they are not formally incompatible but they sit ill together. This constitutes a serious difficulty, not least because Armstrong has recently attempted to prove the correctness of realism, refuting the resemblance theory *en passant* (1978: 44-57). At least one materialist metaphysic looks like a house divided against itself. And if Armstrong's refutation of the resemblance theory is sound (as it seems to me to be) this will be a problem for all topic-neutral theories of mind.

If realism is the correct theory for the generality of qualities and other universals, then those supposed qualities which modify experience (albeit intentionally or adverbially) and which are analysed in terms of similarity will not be genuine qualities at all. The 'gappy' analysis which Armstrong gives for secondary qualities, of which he believes our experience is particularly uninformative, will apply to all qualities. It is not merely that experience so construed does not tell us the nature of the corresponding properties in the external world, but, more strongly, that what constitute the internal objects of experience are not qualities at all. It will not do to say that this was the whole point of topic-neutral analysis, namely to deny the reality of internal objects of awareness, for if the man who hallucinates a yellow lion is not reporting *what his experience seems to be of* then he is reporting nothing. This approach is adopted by some behaviourists and Wittgensteinians, who deny that introspective reports are really reports, saying instead that the reporting and other bits of behaviour are all there is to such experiences.[1] But it is precisely to avoid this implausible treatment of sensation that the idea that we are reporting something *but only topic neutrally* was proposed.

In sum, the argument is as follows. The physicalist, in contrast to the behaviourist, asserts (1) reports of subjective experience are genuine reports; and (2) such reports are topic neutral. Given that (3) what gives its particular character to an experience is its object, then (4) the object is what is topic neutrally reported. As (5) our knowledge of the object of experience will be topic neutral if our reports of it must be neutral, (6) experience only gives us topic-neutral knowledge of its object. As (7) the objects of experience are seeming things and seeming qualities, then (8) experience only gives us topic-neutral

1   The anti-private-language argument is presumably an instance of this.

knowledge of how things and qualities seem. But, (9) Smart explains this topic-neutral knowledge in terms of recognising similarity and dissimilarity. Therefore (10) he gives a resemblance analysis of how things and qualities seem. If (11) qualities and other universals cannot be treated in terms of resemblance but must be treated realistically, then (given (10)) (12) how things and qualities seem cannot be explained by reference to things and qualities understood in their actual (i.e. realistic) nature. But (13) necessarily the analysis of 'F' in 'seems F' must be the same as its analysis in 'is F': if a reductive (e.g. a resemblance) analysis of it is inadequate to one case it ought to be inadequate to the other, for we are dealing with the same quality. Indeed, if they are subject to such radically different analyses they cannot be the same quality. Finally, (14) it is absurd to suppose that the same predicate/property cannot occur in both these contexts.

The topic-neutral approach can only be saved if we reject realist theories of universals; more precisely, the resemblance analysis must be adequate for all those properties which we might ever seem to experience. One way of refuting the theory does not absolutely rule out this possibility. It is commonly argued that, even if the resemblance theory can cope with all other universals, it cannot cope with the universal *resemblance* itself (e.g. Armstrong, 1978: 55). This is the strongest argument against the resemblance theory, but it does leave open the possibility that someone might take what is on offer and accept that there must be *one* universal, namely resemblance, whilst denying that there are any others. This is a possible position but not an attractive one if you were after a unified theory of universals: it is suspiciously *ad hoc*. The intuitive objection to the resemblance theory is that objects are similar *because of* the properties they possess – properties *ground* resemblance, they are not a *construct* from it. Once the need for at least one universal has been conceded it seems natural to throw in the towel and admit that this intuition is sound.

Armstrong's account of secondary qualities shows that he has not noticed the pitfalls of a topic-neutral treatment of experience. Science has no place for secondary qualities and so Armstrong suggests that when we perceive a so-called secondary quality we are not aware of a real quality at all. Our concept of red, for example, 'is all blank or gap' and 'we know *nothing* about what redness is in its own nature ... we only know contingent truths about redness – such truths as that it is a property detected by the eye and possessed ... by such things as

49

the surfaces of ripe tomatoes and Jonathan apples' (1968: 275). We have to await science to tell us what real, primary qualities the surface of an object possesses when we call it red. Armstrong is treating secondary qualities in an explicitly resemblance manner. He compares seeing red things to being able to recognise members of the same family without being aware of how they resemble one another:

> Red objects all have a property in common which all normal observers can detect. But we normal observers are not aware of the nature of this property. We can only identify the property by reference to the way it is detected (by the eyes) and by mentioning objects that happen to be red. What principally stands in the way of our accepting this solution is the illusion that perception gives us a through-and-through knowledge of, or aquaintance with, such qualities as redness. (1968: 276)

Armstrong here accepts that if we perceive something in terms only of its resemblance relations, then we get no hold on the intrinsic nature of the quality. Because he believes that there are no secondary qualities in the world and that our apparent perception of them is just a sort of confused perception of the primary qualities that underlie them, this conclusion is welcome to him in the case of such qualities. It enables him to dispense with some embarrassing entities. But if all our perception is simply the recognition of resemblances, then we will know nothing about the intrinsic nature of any perceivable qualities. The topic-neutral account of experience makes impossible the very distinction between qualities we perceive 'gappily' and those we perceive in some fuller way, in their intrinsic nature. By his own standards, it would seem that Armstrong cannot allow that we ever perceive any real properties at all: our grasp of the nature of every empirical quality is as empty as our direct grasp of the real underlying nature of secondary qualities.

The topic-neutral analysis of experience is openly employed in stimulus materialism and the causal analysis of mind. I argued above in chapter 2.7 that it is also required by functionalism and can therefore conclude something which has often been suspected − though recently denied by Armstrong (1978) − that materialist theories are incompatible with realist theories of universals. The tie between nominalism and materialism is an ancient one; Armstrong has shown that the prospects for nominalism are poor; we can conclude that those for materialism are inevitably no better.

4

The causal theory of mind

I TWO VERSIONS OF THE THEORY

By following the development of behaviourism in the face of various problems, we saw that it is naturally transformed into some form of physicalism. The forms of physicalism to emerge from this process were stimulus materialism and the causal theory of mind. However, a close examination of the stimulus theory has shown that it must inevitably develop in the direction of the causal analysis. The causal theory, therefore, appears to be the natural heir to the whole reductionist tradition of materialist thought.

There are two importantly different versions of the causal approach to the analysis of mind. According to the first, a mental state is whatever state mediates between stimulus and response in a certain sort of way. It is hypothesised that brain states will be found to have this mediatory role. These brain states are, therefore, identical with mental states, and this first version of the causal theory is, consequently, a form of the mind—brain identity theory. According to the second version of the theory, a mental state is a state of the organism as a whole, which that organism possesses in virtue of having some causal state which mediates appropriately between stimulus and response. The mediating state is not, in this case, identical with the mental, but is only the logical foundation of the organism's being in the mental state. This is, therefore, not a form of the mind—brain identity theory. The difference between these theories will be developed in the course of the discussion, and we shall see that it reflects different analyses of dispositional concepts.

Although both theories are versions of the causal analysis of mind, I shall generally reserve the expression 'the causal theory' for the former and call the latter 'functionalism'. The identification of the latter with functionalism is not misleading (see ch. 2.7).[1]

1   Block, 1978, groups together Armstrong, Lewis, Putnam and Fodor (and others) under the title 'functionalist'. I am not clear how acceptable this is to the philosophers involved, but, as my arguments show, it seems to be correct.

Functionalism is a theory which treats mental states as functional states of a creature whose behaviour is sufficiently sophisticated to be interpreted psychologically. The function of mental states is, therefore, to produce behaviour which manifests beliefs, desires, sensory awareness etc. These functional states may be (and, it is presumed, will be) 'realised in' − that is, causally grounded or embodied in − the physical states of the creature, but there is no simple identity between the mental and the physical (Putnam, 1975a). Thus functionalism is a version of the causal theory which eschews mind−brain identity, whilst admitting that the relevant functions supervene on their physical ground.

The differences between these two theories are important for a variety of reasons, but mainly for the following. Reductionist and materialist theories of mind face two problems. First, they have the problem of stating, in materialist or topic-neutral terms, necessary and sufficient conditions for being in certain mental states. For example, we saw that behaviourism could not, within its own terms, pick out just those situations when someone was in pain. Second, they have to make these theories intuitively acceptable by making them true to the phenomena of consciousness. This is not the same problem as stating equivalences. Even if the behaviourist could pick out just those circumstances in which we would agree the subject was genuinely in pain, we might still refuse to agree that behaving in the specified way was all there is to suffering pain. The replacement of behaviourism by a causal theory still leaves these two problems. Even if one could prove a sentence of the form 's is in mental state M iff s is in causal state C' it would remain to make plausible the further claim that C was all there was to being conscious in the way appropriate to M. Armstrong, who propounds the causal theory proper, proposes to solve this phenomenological problem by a theory of introspection according to which consciousness consists in perceiving or 'scanning' those of one's brain states which are in fact identical to mental states. He acknowledges that without this element his theory is hardly less intuitively inadequate than behaviourism (1968: 93 and, more forcefully, 1970: 75f). It is a necessary condition for the truth of such a theory that the mental state and brain state be identical: it looks as if (and we shall investigate this further) the brain state's being the ground of the mental state will not be sufficient for the scanning of the one to be identical with the perceiving of the other.

Therefore, functionalism may well be unable to accommodate the theory of consciousness which the causal theory appears to allow. If, therefore, one is impressed by the need for some doctrine of consciousness in addition to the purely technical causal analysis, it will turn out to be very important that the causal theory, as against functionalism, be the correct theory.

The natural strategy for our discussion is to begin with the causal theory of Armstrong and Lewis and see how, if at all, we are forced to modify it in the face of criticisms. The conclusion at which we will arrive is that the intuitive inadequacies in the behaviourist treatment of consciousness are shared by both versions of the causal theory.

2 AMBIGUITIES IN THE REALIST THEORY OF DISPOSITIONS

Armstrong presents his analysis of mind as follows:

> The concept of a mental state is primarily the concept of *a state of the person apt for bringing about a certain sort of behaviour.* Sacrificing all accuracy for brevity we can say that, although mind is not behaviour, it is the *cause* of behaviour. In the case of some mental states only they are also *states of the person apt for being brought about by a certain sort of stimulus.* But this latter formula is a secondary one. (1968: 82)

As a matter of fact, the states with these causal powers are, it is hypothesised, states of the central nervous system.

The same combination of analytical and empirical premises to generate a materialist conclusion is succinctly expressed by Lewis:

> My argument is this: The definitive characteristic of any (sort of) experience as such is its causal role, its syndrome of most typical causes and effects. But we materialists believe that those causal roles which belong by analytical necessity to experiences belong in fact to certain physical states. Since those physical states possess the definitive characteristics of experience, they must be the experiences. (1966: 17)

This causal theory is strictly an identity theory, for it says that the *neural* state with the appropriate causal role simply is the mental state. The central nervous system and its states considered in their own right, without further context, are identical with the mind and its states. This leads Armstrong to claim that he can accommodate certain dualist intuitions of a sort normally rejected by philosophers who connect the identity of mental states with their behavioural functions. For example, he believes that he can accommodate the logical possibility of inverted spectra, the logical possibility that

53

your pains feel like my tickles, and the logical possibility of disembodied minds (1968: 256-60, 91). All these things are possible because just that sort of brain state which in me is my seeing something red might in you be your seeing something green; those in you when you are hurt may be in me when I am tickled; and the whole central nervous system could be stored without the rest of the body and so be, in a sense, a 'disembodied' mind. Considered in the light of the causal theory itself these seem dubious claims. If what makes a state mental is its possession of a certain causal role, then what mental state it is identical with presumably depends on what causal role it possesses. The mentality consists in the causal properties of the brain. It is, therefore, rational to regard states with the same relevant causal properties as identical *qua* mental and those with different causal properties as different *qua* mental.

There are three ways of stating the materialist version of the causal criterion and Armstrong shows insufficient awareness of the differences. One might say,

(1) Mental state M is identical with neurological state s, or
(2) Mental state M is identical with certain causal properties of neurological state s, or
(3) Mental state M is identical with a dispositional state which a person possesses in virtue of neurological state s.

(3) is functionalism as we defined it above. It can also be regarded as a special case of (2), for the disposition of the whole organism is, in a sense, equivalent to the remote causal properties of s. To separate (2) and (3) more definitely, we can understand (2) as referring to the more immediate causal properties of s; for example, ones that might be expressed in neurological terms. Thus,

(2′) Mental state M is identical with certain immediate causal properties of neurological state s.

Failure to take note of these three ways of expressing causal materialism rests upon a parallel failure to notice different ways of stating the realist theory of dispositions. Armstrong characterises his causal theory as behaviourism with a realist theory of dispositions. According to traditional or 'Rylean' behaviourism, to possess a mental state is to possess a certain disposition and this latter is 'not to be in a particular state, or to undergo a particular change; it is to be bound or liable to be in a particular state, or to undergo a particular change, when a particular condition is realised' (Ryle, 1949: 43).

On this theory, dispositions are not causes and do not essentially involve internal causes; rather they involve only some correlation between circumstances and performances. The realist theory of dispositions, on the other hand, asserts that to possess a disposition is to have some internal state which causes one to behave as disposed. Thus, on the Rylean theory, to say that glass is brittle is to say that there has been in the past a correlation between its being struck and its breaking, and to affirm one's faith that this correlation will continue, whereas on the realist theory to say that glass is brittle is to say that there is some structural feature of glass which causes it to break easily when struck. By applying the realist theory to the philosophy of mind, Rylean behaviourism automatically transforms itself into some sort of causal or functionalist theory; for whereas originally the presence of a disposition carried no consequences for the internal workings of the person, on the realist theory it does involve commitment to the presence of an internal structure which causes the behaviour which we ascribe to the disposition. Armstrong, however, does not merely say that the existence of a disposition entails the existence of an internal or structural cause; he says that the disposition is identical with the structural cause (1968: 88). In fact he seems to take this latter manner of expression as the natural way of expressing a realist theory of dispositions. In so doing he fails sufficiently to distinguish three variants on the realist theory of dispositions which parallel those on the causal theory of mind.

(4) Disposition D of body B is identical with internal structure T.
(5) Disposition D of body B is identical with certain immediate causal properties of structure T.
(6) Disposition D of body B is a state B possesses in virtue of (the causal properties of) some internal structure T.

All three are realist because they all take it that the existence of a disposition entails the existence of an internal cause, but (6) does not identify the disposition with that internal cause. Armstrong does not think (4) and (5) are interestingly different, for he wants to say that the relation between the intrinsic and causal properties of a structure is one of mutual entailment (1969-70). I shall not here discuss this very difficult issue, but it is enough to notice that, although it may be true that no two intrinsically different structures could have all their causal properties in common (nor two intrinsically identical ones possess different powers) any particular

55

causal property might be found in various different structures. Thus, as only some of the powers of central nervous system structures will be relevant to their mental function, it would seem that, according to (5), different structures might meet the same role. And once we reach remote causal properties of the sort referred to in (6), then the variety of structures that could in theory fill the role will be considerable. If one regards (4) and (5) as necessarily co-extensive (as, we have just pointed out, Armstrong does) and then fails to notice the difference between (5) and (6), one will fail to see that the disposition which belongs to the body as a whole is not identical with the structure most central to its grounding, nor to the immediate causal properties of that structure. How closely related an internal structure is to a disposition will depend on how much extra machinery is necessary before it can have the appropriate consequence. In so far as a central structure depends on more peripheral connexions, a change in the latter could entirely alter the identity of the disposition which the structure grounds. Such is the versatility of a steam engine that, if appropriately connected to four wheels, it is the structure which grounds a capacity for locomotion; but if it is connected into a different system it grounds the entirely different capacity for pumping water out of mineshafts. This versatility must, in principle, apply to any mechanical part short of the complete system.

Such structures cannot, therefore, be identified with the dispositions of the complete systems, even though they are the principle or central ground for that disposition.

This fact has grievous consequences for Armstrong's conception of himself as a Cartesian materialist. He believes that the central nervous system is the complete mind, like the Cartesian mental substance. Consequently, he thinks, he can accommodate such Cartesian intuitions as the logical possibility of disembodied minds. For Armstrong this simply means a brain without the rest of the body. Armstrong believes that an artificial brain or central nervous system which was stimulated so as to produce states similar to those found in normal people when they are having experiences would have experiences itself. The behaviourist could ascribe mental events to it only in counterfactual terms, but the physicalist can ascribe categorical mental events to it. Thus physicalism is shown to be superior to behaviourism (1968: 76, 91). I presume that Armstrong would extend what he says about an artificial brain to a disembodied but natural brain. However, not merely is it the case that such a creature would have no actual mental life on Armstrong's theory, but it would not even have one single, or probably any determinate number, of counterfactual mental lives.

By the formula 'This brain state is contingently identical with an intention to F' Armstrong suggests that the tendency to produce F-ing is a property of the brain state itself, as much as are its other, purely physical, causal powers. We do assume that what an intention is an intention to do is part and parcel of that intention — indeed it is its essence. However, the brain state only has the causal consequences of F-ing, given much more causal apparatus. I am not merely saying that more is needed for the intention to be carried out, but that the rest of the apparatus has to be as it is for that brain state to be the intention to F; so that, if certain muscular connexions in a limb were reversed, that brain state which in fact represents the intention to lower the arm would represent the intention to raise it. This could be generalised to all types of mental state. I think that this fact renders vacuous Armstrong's claim that on his theory a disembodied brain could have a mind, because it would have all sorts of behavioural tendencies. Such a brain would be a very woolly mind, for what desires and intentions it had would be almost wholly determinable, and dependent on the structure of the indefinite number of mechanisms into which it might be inserted.

In reply it might be said that the brain *must* be considered relative to a normal human body. Clearly this is the most reasonable assumption for a *behaviourist* to make when describing what purely counterfactual mental states such a brain would possess, for, as the states in question are not being taken as actual, the most convenient standard of comparison is with the most commonly known form of embodiment. But for the central state materialist no counterfactual reference should be required at all, just as it is not for the Cartesian. The identity of certain mental states at least is entirely independent of extra-mental context on both these theories.

Any difficulty of conceiving of a human brain in a very different body, such that exactly similar states produce different effects, is a purely practical one, and a question of complexity: the general principle that the same motor might drive a vehicle forwards or backwards by precisely the same internal workings, depending on what sort of mechanism it is fitted into, needs no defence, and the physicalist conception of man requires that, even allowing for laws emergent at the biological level, the system is mechanistic in this way. There might even be creatures with humanoid brains, but different bodies; we might *in fact* differ, in certain respects (e.g. connexions between muscles) in the way mentioned above. Even the whole body will not possess a determinate mental state solely in virtue of its internal structure independently of its environment, for its causally relevant powers may vary with that environment. The most striking case of this would be the existence of creatures with bodies almost exactly like ours, except that they were naturally incarcerated in a further 'outer body' which, by its muscle connexions, reversed the impact of movements of the 'inner body'.

Perhaps a weaker position is tenable; namely that a disembodied central nervous system which had once had a body could possess a mental life of the sort appropriate to the type of body that was in fact its own. But this again would be no more than a convenient convention; for if the central nervous system could be transferred to another and different style of body which it inhabited without showing behavioural signs of frustration (which, given the mechanical conception of the central nervous system, must be theoretically possible), then there would be no grounds for saying that it had an *actual* mental life appropriate to the one rather than the other.

3 THE LIMITS OF MENTAL REPRESENTATION

Armstrong's identity theory is a type—type theory: that is, he holds that there are law-like connexions between types of mental and types of physical states. Accordingly one could say that all pains of a certain sort are identical with a type of neurological event: every instance of that sort of pain is identical with an instance of that sort of brain process, and vice versa. This is essential to Armstrong's claim that he can allow inverted spectra or that what it is like for dogs to see might be different from what it is like for humans to see. In these cases the type of neural state normally associated with a given experience occurs in the wrong context (or fails to occur at all): so, Armstrong says, the experience had is different.

Opponents of type—type identity argue that it is very unlikely that the state which houses something as abstract as a belief or

58

concept should be similar between people. They are probably more willing to accept the likelihood of similarity in the embodiments of sensations, at least within a species. The crucial point, however, is not that such similarity is unlikely, but that it is irrelevant. Putnam has pointed out that the same program can be embodied in different forms of hardware and that, on taking a cybernetic analogy for human intelligence, there is no reason why the same should not be true of psychic functions (1975b: 435-7). This analogy with computers only cuts ice if mental states can be characterised without relevant remainder in functional terms. It is difficult to see how this could be so unless they were reductively analysable in such terms.

The crucial functionalist point is not that there must be or even that there are differences between the central physical states most closely corresponding to certain mental states, but that the central state alone would not count as the mental state because its function depends on its context. This is what leaves open the possibility that different systems might embody the same mental state in different ways. There is in fact a range of options being disputed. The strongest anti-type—type theory is that, even within one and the same creature, there need not be any interesting internal physical similarity between two embodiments of the same mental or functional state.

Hartry Field (1978) has argued against the latter thesis on the grounds that propositional attitudes involve relations to propositions and a physicalist account of such a relation must take the form of some relation to an internal physical analogue of a sentence. Something could not be the representation of a sentence, given the importance of structure for sentences, unless it betrayed a high degree of representational regularity. Field's argument is appealing, but even if true does not affect the issues in which we are interested. This is so because even if there are internal representations of sentences corresponding to the propositional content of our thoughts, these internal representations cannot be identified with the thoughts or their contents. An analogous argument can be given. It would not be possible to record a piece of music without making marks on a disc which corresponded nomically to the musical phrases one was recording. Different types of recording might involve different forms of representation, but within a particular recording a consistent form of representation is obviously required. This is parallel to Field's argument. However, the marks on a disc are not music. They are neither music in the sense in which a score is music, for that is a sign system with non-natural meaning; nor, more obviously, are they actual musical sounds. They are physical marks on structures which, when placed in the context of certain further physical apparatus (e.g. a gramophone), will produce music. This parallels fairly exactly the sense in which neural representation is not identical with mental content: it can be called 'mental representation' if one means by that that it represents or maps what is in the mind, but not if it is supposed to *be* the mental presence (of the proposition) itself.

I do not wish to claim that the point to which I am drawing attention is the only important difference between functionalism and the causal theory. I am claiming only that the central state depends on its context to constitute the mental state in such a way that the central state itself cannot be said to be identical with the mental state. The point is exactly similar to that about disposition: the realist foundation of a disposition is not identical with the disposition.

4 KRIPKE AND THE IDENTITY THEORY

Kripke's argument against the identity theory reinforces and extends the conclusions we have so far reached (1972: 334-42). He argues that, properly understood, all identity statements necessarily have the truth-value they do. An identity statement such as

(1) Benjamin Franklin is identical with the inventor of bifocals

can be interpreted in either of two ways. First, one could interpret both referring expressions as rigid designators − that is, as designating the same individual object in all possible worlds. 'Benjamin Franklin', being a proper name, is naturally taken in this way, for the purpose of this name is to pick out just that particular individual; it is not a description under which different things might have fallen if circumstances had been different. By contrast, 'the inventor of bifocals' is a description which might, in different worlds, have been satisfied by different people; someone other than Franklin might have invented bifocals. However, 'the inventor of bifocals' can quite easily be taken rigidly as simply a way of referring to Franklin. Using it in this sense we can say,

(2) The inventor of bifocals might not have invented bifocals, for it is plainly correct that the inventor of bifocals − Franklin − might not have invented bifocals.

Taking both designators rigidly, (1) expresses a necessary truth, for it is equivalent to

(3) Benjamin Franklin is identical with the inventor of bifocals,

i.e. with Franklin:

which is just another way of saying that Franklin is identical with Franklin; this is of the form $a = a$ and is obviously necessary.

Alternatively one might interpret the description non-rigidly, that is, as designating different objects in different worlds. On this interpretation

(4) Benjamin Franklin might not have been identical with the inventor of bifocals

is true. However, (4) is not a particularly natural way of expressing what it appears to say. It is more natural to say simply

(5) Benjamin Franklin might not have invented bifocals.

Similarly, the indicative affirmative is more naturally not expressed in the identity form, but as

(6) Benjamin Franklin invented bifocals.

Thus, when the description 'the inventor of bifocals' is meant non-rigidly (1) means no more than (6).

The identity theorist subscribes to propositions such as

(7) Smith's feeling pain is identical with his c-fibres firing.

Kripke says that if (7) is true it is necessarily true, because it is an identity statement. But, he says, it is obviously not necessary, for we could imagine Smith having that very brain state and yet feeling nothing: therefore (7) is not true.

Someone might argue that this imagining does not represent a real possibility. We have already seen, in chapter 2.2, Peacocke take this line and shown that his argument is unsound, although Peacocke is not a reductionist and so cannot call into play the following difficulty for Kripke's argument. Might it not be the case that if one allows that mental and physical properties are different, then one cannot deny that one could be instantiated without the other, but that if one *reduces* mental properties to physical ones, then it does not make sense to suggest that there could be the one without the other? Intuitively it is clear why someone might think this, for if there is no analytic or translational connexion between mental and physical predicates, then it looks as if the presence of any physical properties in the absence of any mental properties should be a possibility. However, on the same principle, if one gives a physicalist, behaviourist or topic-neutral analysis of mental predicates, so that mental properties turn out to be physical properties, then it looks as if the relevant physical states could not be present without the accompanying mental ones (with which they are identical). Can the reductionist therefore avoid Kripke's argument? If, for example, one thought that feeling pain were just to be in a certain state apt to cause pain-behaviour, then a mere physical system could have such a causal state and therefore be in pain. It would not be possible for there to be a physical system just like that, including its causal properties, in a normal context and it not be in pain, according to the analysis of pain provided by the causal theory.

However, we need now to distinguish two forms of reductive physicalism, for Kripke is not attacking reductive physicalism in general but only the identity theory. Functionalism and behaviourism are reductive theories, but do not identify mental states with particular physical states or processes. Reductive versions of the identity theory do not escape Kripke's argument. It is true that, by causal standards, a system with the appropriate causal tendencies would be a person in pain. This does not get us to the point of identifying some state of that system with the person's feeling pain. We have an overall identity of person with total organism, but no identities between particular mental and physical states. And such identities will not be possible, in view of the considerations invoked in earlier sections. Thus if we ask whether c-fibres could have fired just then and yet there have been no pain, the answer must be affirmative, because c-fibre firing would not have constituted a state apt to cause pain-behaviour if other parts of the system had not been constructed as they are, which is quite possible. The firing of the c-fibres might not have occurred in that sort of context; therefore they might not have had the appropriate causal properties; and therefore they might not have been identical with pain. Hence the identity is not necessary and therefore there is no identity.

Someone might reply that this only shows that some other c-fibre firing might not have been a pain and therefore that there is not a type—type identity between c-fibre firing and feelings of pain: it does not show that this firing could have failed to be identical with a feeling of pain, because if other things had been different it would not have been this very firing. It is difficult to discuss this objection definitively because it is difficult to imagine a compelling criterion for the individuation of firings. However, we can imagine that same organism with some differences in its construction such that the

62

same sort of neural event had different consequences: and if 'c-fibre firing' is a neurological, not psychological, description, we can imagine such as event occurring just at the same time as it did in fact occur and in the same matter, though with a different causal significance for the organism as a whole. So if 'that very firing' means an event of that type in just that parcel of matter at that time then that very firing could have occurred without being a state apt to produce pain-behaviour.

Armstrong's failure to distinguish immediate from remote causal properties leads him into trouble against Kripke. The physical power of the c-fibre firing cannot be identified with any behavioural aptitude of the organism as a whole because the latter is dependent on much more than the causal properties of the former; therefore the latter could have occurred without the former.

We can conclude that (7) cannot be correct.

The situation is no better if one states (7) in terms of the causal theory. Consider:

(8) A feeling of pain is identical with whatever state is apt to produce pain-behaviour.

(8) gives an Armstrongian account of the sensation of pain. Kripke's objections to the mind—brain identity theory apply equally to this topic-neutral analysis. A feeling of pain can be identical with some state apt to produce behaviour only if they could not have failed to be identical. But, as was argued above, whatever state happened to have that causal aptitude could have lacked it. The analysis in (8) might seem sound provided that the state in question is taken to be the whole causal apparatus responsible for pain-behaviour, rather than merely a central state. But this will not do. First, it will not do because it is not plausible to say that muscle connexions are part of a mental state. Second, we have argued in section 2 that the whole body could, if further encased, have had a different behavioural significance. Therefore, some physical apparatus could be identical with the aptitude for pain-behaviour only with the proviso that there is no further relevant apparatus. This negative condition does not extend the content of the identity, in the way that including the afferent system as well as the central nervous system extends it: the *absence* of the further apparatus is not part of what is identical with the feeling. So even the whole system considered in terms of its causal powers is not *identical* with some mental state, for it could have lacked that causal

significance if it had been a part of some further apparatus.

It is clear then that if both the pain and the c-fibres are rigidly designated in (7), then (7) is false, for the identity is not necessary. Should we say then that the designation of pains is not rigid? If we do so we can interpret (7) in a way analogous to that in which (1) is interpreted to produce (6), giving

(9) s's firing c-fibres feel painful.

(6) and (9) are not identity statements and therefore the necessity of identities does not apply. (6) permits the counterfactual

(10) This inventor might not have been an inventor.

And it might seem that (9) similarly permits

(11) This pain might not have hurt (been a pain).

In these sentences the expressions 'this inventor' and 'this pain' do not designate something which is essentially an inventor or something which is essentially a pain. They might be more fully expressed as

(12) This man who is an inventor might not have been an inventor

and

(13) This state which happens to hurt (be a pain) might not have hurt (been a pain).

For this paraphrase to be satisfactory, 'this pain' has to be equivalent to 'this state which is hurting me' and *a pain* to be *something which hurts*. This account of pain has been adopted by certain philosophers. Wiggins (1974: 331), for example, identifies the pain with the state which, contingently, hurts me.[2] He claims that the following arguments are parallel:

(i) Heat is the cause of the sensation of heat

and

(ii) Molecular agitation is the cause of the sensation of heat, therefore

(iii) Heat is molecular agitation;

and

(iv) Pain is what affects us painfully

and

---

2 Maxwell, 1978, takes 'this pain' as rigidly designating a sensation or sensible quality, while scientific descriptions such as 'is a firing c-fibre' non-rigidly ascribe topic-neutral functional properties. This gives a neutral monist account of matter very like that which Lockwood, 1981, ascribes to Russell. See Lockwood for both an explanation of this theory and an account of the problems inherent in it. Such neutral monism is also relevant to the discussion of matter in ch. 7.3 and 7.5.

(v) Neural state *n* is what affects us painfully,
therefore
(vi) Being in pain at time *t* is being in neural state *n* at time *t*.
But (iv) is false in the relevant sense of 'pain'. It is wrong to distinguish between pain and the hurting or being affected painfully which
Wiggins says is what pain causes. The pain is not that which hurts
me, in a sense which separates it from my feeling pain or being
painfully affected. Ironically, this is a point often made by anti-
dualists who remark that there are strictly no such things as pains,
only states of being-in-pain or hurting. Nevertheless, if anyone
wants to take 'pain' in Wiggins's sense, that does not affect Kripke's
argument, for what we will then be interested in will be the *hurting* of
the pain, the being painfully affected, for that is the experiential state
with which the materialist must cope. If we replace (iv) by
(vii) The mental state is our being affected painfully,
this together with (v) only allows us to conclude that the neural state
is what causes the mental state, which is a dualistic, not a materialistic, conclusion.
  What this shows is that 'this pain' in (11) refers not to the same
thing as 's's firing c-fibres' in (9), but to what might variously be
expressed as 's's-firing-c-fibres-feeling-painful', or 'the feeling painful of s's firing c-fibres', or 's's firing c-fibres *qua* feeling painful'.
That is, it refers not just to what affects us painfully, but to our being
painfully affected. This shows a radical disanalogy between (6) and
(10) on the one hand, and (9) and (11) on the other. 'This inventor' in
(10) does designate the same thing as 'Benjamin Franklin' designates
in (6); it does not designate *Benjamin Franklin qua inventing*, or *the
inventing of Benjamin Franklin*, or *Benjamin Franklin inventing*. Therefore (9) does not license (11) in the way that (6) licenses (10), for it is
not true that this pain — that is, s's-firing-c-fibres-feeling-painful
(etc.) — might not have hurt.
  The point is not altered if one restates the argument using the
causal theorist's analysis of pain. For (9) we read
(9') s's firing c-fibres are apt to produce pain-behaviour;
for (11) we read
(11') These firing c-fibres might not have been apt to produce
      pain-behaviour.
The objection remains that (11') does not stand to (9') as (10) does to
(6) because the pain is not just the firing c-fibre, but the firing-c-
fibre-apt- (or *qua*-apt-) to-produce-pain-behaviour. Only then is it

experienced as pain and therefore is the relevant state of consciousness. Thus the correct causal version of (11) would be

(11'') The firing-c-fibre, *qua* apt-to-produce-pain-behaviour, might not have been apt to produce pain-behaviour.

This is a contradiction. It is like

(10')This inventor, *qua* inventor, might not have been an inventor.

(These latter two sentences might seem very odd. Perhaps they are not contradictions but ill-formed. This does not adversely affect the argument, for it means that the attempt to state the identity theory in terms which allow the possibility that those states might not have been mental ends in nonsense instead of in contradiction.)

As there is no acceptable interpretation of (11), then pains are essentially pains and (9) is not a more accurate statement of the theory than (7). In fact (7) was what identity theorists probably intended and (7), we have seen, is false.

These arguments show in what way Armstrong's theory is false. To say that a mental state is identical with *the state apt to produce* the behaviour is incorrect. The mental state is the aptitude, capacity, tendency or disposition for the behaviour. This distinction Armstrong blurs by conflating intrinsic properties and causal properties of a physical system (as was shown in section 2), but it is an essential distinction, for on the causal theory the mind is a collection of causal powers. If one tries to identify that mental state with a cause rather than a causal power, one is blocked by Kripke's argument.

Consider:

(14) A feeling of pain is identical with a causal power (aptitude etc.) to produce pain-behaviour.

This does not fall to Kripke's argument. For this causal power is not identical with the causal properties of any of the apparatus in which it is realised, nor is it, for the reasons given immediately above, identical with the physical causal properties of the system as a whole. It is a property of the system as a whole, in a given context, interpreted psychologically. It is not identical with any of the physical properties of the physical system. This is not to say that it need be an emergent non-physical power. What Kripke's argument shows is that the functionalist, rather than identity theorist, way of expressing the causal analysis is correct: it also corresponds to the third of our realist characterisations of dispositions. For whereas a disposition, aptitude or tendency can properly be said to be housed, embodied or realised in some physical apparatus it cannot be said to be identical with it, or even with the most central part of it. Some parts play a more central role in that realisation than others, just as some parts of a computer play a central role in certain of its capacities, but the capacity itself is not identical with nor realised in that part alone: it may be realised in the system as a whole, though it is not strictly identical even with · that.

5 THE INCOMPATIBILITY OF FUNCTIONALISM AND ARMSTRONG'S THEORY OF CONSCIOUSNESS

If what has been said above is correct, then the identity theory or central state materialism is false. Mental states are not brain states, though brain states may be the most crucial grounding for the possession of mental states. The latter, however, will be dispositions or capacities of the organism as a whole. Thus our argument leads to a weak realist theory of dispositions: that is, one which does not involve identifying a disposition with its causal basis. If we adopt this theory of dispositions, many of the intuitive objections which central state materialists bring against behaviourism will also hold against the causal theory. Dispositions, on the weak realist theory, are just as much abstract or constructed entities as they are on the 'phenomenalist' theory employed by Ryle. For an object to possess a disposition is still for certain conditionals and counterfactuals to be true of it, though it becomes necessary that they are true of it in virtue of certain structural facts. This means that Armstrong's principal objections to behaviourism still stand against the functionalist form of the causal theory which has emerged from our discussion. Armstrong objects that:

Most implausibly, the Behaviourist denies the existence of *inner* mental processes. There seems to be more going on in us than mere outward physical behaviour ... (1968: 57)

Is 'calculation in the head' little more than a period of silence followed by an intelligent answer? At least sometimes when we 'calculate in our heads' are we not aware of a *current event*: something that goes on in us at the time of the calculation? And what account can the Behaviourist give of this happening? By hypothesis, it is not a piece of overt behaviour. It may be replied that during the 'calculation' we were disposed to say and do certain things, and that we were afterwards able to report the existence of these dispositions. But granting this, was there not something *actual* going on, of which we were aware at the time? (ibid.: 69)

Armstrong's intuitive objection to behaviourism is, therefore, that it does not allow mental events to be actual, current and internal events. This 'concreteness' is supposedly provided by the central state materialist account of mental events. But if the current, actual and internal central events are not in fact identical with the mental events, then Armstrong's well founded dissatisfaction with behaviourism still remains against the physicalism which has emerged from the causal analysis.

As was suggested in section 1 of this chapter, the possibility of improving on the behaviourist's empty account of consciousness is removed by this functionalist version of the causal theory. The view of consciousness as awareness of something 'actual' and 'internal' is destroyed by the restoration of dispositions to their previous status as abstract entities, albeit with categorical foundations. This point is reinforced by a closer look at Armstrong's account of how we were supposed to perceive our internal 'central state' mental events. Because they are causal tendencies, perception of them is analogous to perceiving or feeling pressure: we do not *see* causal properties directly, but we can *feel* them. Armstrong says, 'it seems that touch involves a direct, or non-inferential awareness of causes. Here is a perceptual parallel to the awareness of causal relation that our account attributes to "inner sense" ' (1968: 97). He recognises that it is essential to the plausibility of his account that such tactile perception is non-inferential and does not consist, for example, of the awareness of a sensation plus a learnt knowledge that such sensations are generally followed by bodily movements. But if our preceding arguments are sound, a similar inference will be involved in introspection, for it is contingent that the causal properties of processes within the central nervous system have some particular significance for the organism as a whole: the 'pressure', if identified with the intra-brain causal properties of some brain process, will not have a non-inferentially graspable significance for the body as a whole, but will depend on further contingent facts about its housing. Only someone with independent access to those other facts could infer the significance of the brain states he was scanning.

A simple conclusion follows: that although the 'monitoring' or 'scanning' of one part of the brain by another may map, mirror or ground self-consciousness, it cannot be identical with it.

I have tried to show that the causal theory must retreat into a form of functionalism and that that theory cannot support the self-scanning model of consciousness. Before passing some final comments on functionalism I wish to prove that, even within the framework of the causal theory proper, this model of consciousness would be inadequate. The following arguments against this model of introspection and consciousness seem particularly strong.

(1) That introspection is literally a scanning device is surely improbable, for scanning is the emitting of some ray or beam from one object in one place and its lighting upon and reflecting off some other object at another place, so that information regarding the object acted upon can be gained by the object acting. It would be absurd to assume *a priori* that such radar-like activities occur in the brain. The essence of perception, for Armstrong, is that an object or a state of affairs acts upon a person in such a way as to produce in him the disposition for an appropriate behavioural response. According to an Armstrongian theory of perception, then, all that need occur in the brain for introspection to be perception, is for the state introspected to bring about some further state with the property of causing behaviour appropriate to being conscious of being in the initial state. Further elaboration of the relationship between the state introspecting and that introspected runs unnecessarily the danger of empirical falsification.

However, the scanning analogy looks as if it was imported to make the process in question look more like a form of perception, *as perception is normally conceived of*, than, on Armstrong's theory, it is. By stressing the activity of the scanning state, the scanner and the scanned are put into a clear relation that looks rather like that of perceiver and perceived. We have a natural tendency to regard perception as an activity rather than mere receptivity, but for normal perception, where perceiver and object perceived are (usually) clearly separate objects, the fact that a mainly passive analysis of perception may be found necessary does not seriously harm the autonomy and separateness of the perceiver and perceived; it is clear where the process begins and where it ends. There is no such clear separateness (e.g. no empty, transparent space) between the two brain states. If we take state A as being that appropriate to subliminally perceiving state of affairs s, and state z as being that appropriate, when caused by

A, to the fully conscious perception of s, then why should not all the states on the causal chain between A and z have the capacity of producing some greater degree of sophistication, and self-conscious-like response to s? Then what we would have is not two discrete behaviour-producing states, but an initial minimal state A and many other behaviour-producing states which A can (under appropriate circumstances) cause to be activated, right up to the point where normal fully conscious behavioural readiness is induced. This supposition is not artificial, for there is something like a continuum of increasingly self-conscious behaviour. On this interpretation, is each state a perception of the one immediately previous to it, or are they all perceptions of A, or are they all perceptions of all those previous to them, or is z alone a perception of A? Whilst the theory is couched in terms of perception these seem to be real questions, but if one understands it in its completely 'reduced' neo-behaviourist form, it is clear that these are not real questions. The only facts are that a series of causal states are responsible for additional complexities in the response-capacity. This shows how attenuated is Armstrong's comparison between introspection and perception: as this process seems to meet his criteria for perception his theory of perception is also shown to be weak.

It seems then that Armstrong's theory gives rise to problems about the individuation of introspective acts and of their (intentional) objects. It will be objected that we can speak of a computer monitoring its own states and therefore we must be able to make sense of the model for humans. But this does not follow, for three reasons. First, although we may be able to identify the state monitored, can we identify a *particular* state — as opposed to a process issuing in some output — which counts as *the* monitoring or of that which is monitored? Second, the behaviour of the computer is simple; there is only one basic type of response that expresses monitoring and thus the process seems to be a simple, two-level perceiver—perceived situation. But there are many degrees of sophistication and self-consciousness of human response, as said above. If the computer were just as complex it would be just as impossible to regard its self-monitoring on a discrete perceptual model. Third, the assessment of a machine's performance as a case of self-monitoring is essentially external and based on our views of what the machine is for and our consequent interpretation of its output. But in our case self-awareness is not a matter of external evaluation but something

70

that reveals itself to the subject: that something is a piece of human self-monitoring cannot be regarded as a piece of interpretation, from an external viewpoint, of the performance.

(2) Another objection concerns a particularly interesting, though essentially different, version of the difficulties with intentional objects and is raised by the assimilation of full perceptual consciousness to introspection. We are told that the difference between perceiving something subliminally and perceiving it fully consciously is that in the latter case one is introspecting one's perception – that is, when fully analysed, the perception is of the causal properties of a brain state. To suggest that the difference consists in perception of my behavioural tendencies does not seem to fit the phenomena: when I suddenly become conscious of the red light at which I have already automatically stopped, what it seems to me I suddenly became aware of is the light, not my own behavioural tendencies (or at least, not only my behavioural tendencies). If I were reporting the event I would probably say something like this: 'And I suddenly realised that there was a traffic light in front of me' or 'Suddenly I saw (noticed) this traffic light.' Even if I did report my behaviour, it would be in conjunction with reporting the light – 'I realised that I had stopped at this red light' – it was not that I had just realised that I had stopped, although I was previously fully aware of the light, though not of perceiving it or responding to it. Thus when I suddenly became fully conscious, from having been acting automatically, I became fully conscious of the object of my initial perception, not just of my being disposed to react to it. I do not see how perception of one's act of perceiving could present itself phenomenally as a heightening of consciousness of the object of perception. (This is particularly true given that introspection is interpreted on analogy with touch, as awareness of pressure, and not with sight.)

(3) Furthermore, on Armstrong's theory the following situation should not make sense. I am aware of having tendencies to behave in all the ways appropriate to driving down a busy street and I am in fact caused to have these tendencies by my situation as a driver in a busy street, but do not seem to be aware of (e.g. do not seem to see) any objects around me. If Armstrong's theory is correct, being caused by objects to have the appropriate dispositions towards them counts as perceiving them and having the appropriate dispositions towards these initial tendencies counts as being introspectively aware of my perception. Therefore, the caveat 'But I do not seem to be aware of

the objects' ought to produce only nonsense. However, the thought experiment above seems to make good sense: I could be made aware of what I was inclined to do without being aware of what was inclining me to do it. It could seem to me that I was inclined to behave as if a traffic light had changed to red in front of me without seeming to be aware of a traffic light. Therefore, Armstrong's theory does not capture the proper object of the perception.

Moreover, that the difference between conscious and subliminal perception does not consist in perceiving one's own tendencies to behave is clearly shown by considering the circumstances under which we can learn and consciously 'cash' our concepts. These circumstances under which someone learns and standardly shows (especially to himself) that he has some empirical concept are conditions of full consciousness. I could hardly teach someone the meaning of 'red' or 'traffic light' by referring him to occasions on which he had subliminally reacted to red traffic lights. I am not saying that someone cannot be taught or conditioned subliminally, but someone who was so taught and who also used his knowledge only unselfconsciously, would not know what he knew and would not show the ability to report which goes with normal human knowledge of empirical concepts. Subliminal teaching is a more complex, derivative and less central case than fully conscious teaching. Without some preparation, such as hypnosis, we can't point something out to someone without drawing his attention to it — making him fully conscious of it. How could this fact (i.e. the dependence of learning on full consciousness) be explained if such consciousness had as its object, not something which instantiated the concept that one was acquiring, but a state of one's own behavioural readiness?

This point can be brought out by considering the case of hallucination. Suppose someone hallucinates a large square. Then he will have two relevant brain states: first, the brain state that normally goes with perceiving a square, and second, that which constitutes introspecting the first. The only *actual* thing of which the subject is aware is the brain state identical with his initial disposition to respond as if there were a square present; however, the experience is plainly not simply one of being aware of *feeling inclined to behave as if there were a square*, but it is an experience as of a square. There is no way in which someone could mistake for a square his tendency to respond as if there were a square, and yet the hallucinating subject does mistake the content of his experience for a square. There are two ways in which one might try to cope with this problem. (i) It might be argued that hallucinating a square is just being disposed to report and behave as if there were a square. This theory differs in no essential way from the traditional behaviourist approach. The improvement that central state materialism supposedly makes possible, namely that there is something actual going on in the mind which can be the object of awareness, is lost. (ii) One might follow Smart and build the apparent objects of awareness into the brain state, and then claim that one only recognises them as similar to or dissimilar from others. But this theory has already been refuted.

In summary of the last two objections to the self-perceiving theory of consciousness we can say that the same theory which accounts for awareness of a psychological state will not also explain 'fully conscious awareness' of an external object. Introspection (e.g. being aware of feeling angry) and being fully aware of the external world are different phenomena. One cannot do what Armstrong wants to do, namely account for fully conscious awareness by summing subliminal awareness of the external world and subliminal awareness that one is aware.

(4) These considerations suggest another argument, which appears to be valid though it is somewhat dramatic. Berkeley has various arguments which purport to show that the notions of an unperceived material object or unperceived quality are incoherent. One of his arguments (*Principles*, section 23) is that, as we always perceive objects being perceived we perceive them *qua* perceived, and thus from perception we can form no conception of them as unperceived. His claim is that part of the intentional content by means of which objects are grasped in consciousness is *that they are perceived*. To imagine an object unperceived is to imagine it as not being an object of consciousness and this he supposes to involve a contradiction; namely that the object both is an object of consciousness (by dint of being imagined) and is not. His argument is fallacious, for it confuses the truism that for something to be imagined it must be an object of consciousness with the falsehood that it must be imagined under the aspect of being, or *as*, an object of consciousness. However, in so far as our conceiving of the world depends on our perceiving it, Berkeley's argument for idealism would be sound if it really were true that we perceive things *as* perceived. The disturbing consequence for the causal theorist is that Berkeley's argument is valid in the context of their doctrines of

73

perception and introspection. Armstrong asserts these two premises:

    (1) For quality F to be an object of s's full consciousness is for s to be (introspectively) aware of being aware of something F.

    (2) All awareness is propositional: that is, it is awareness *that* …

From these can be derived

    (3) For quality F to be the object of s's full consciousness is for s to be aware that he is aware that something is F.

Which is to say that

    (4) The intentional content of any act of full consciousness of some quality includes the characterisation that the quality is an object of awareness.

The controversial step in the argument will be (4), for (1) is the assertion of Armstrong's doctrine of introspection and (2) is his theory of perception, whilst (3) follows incontroversially from them. But (4) might seem to be an unclear interpretation of (3). To see that (4) is a sound interpretation of (3) consider the following transformations. We can move from

    (i)   s is aware that x is F

to its equivalent

    (ii) s aware of x as (*qua*) F.

If we take as the statement of introspective awareness

    (iii) s is aware that s is aware of something F,

then, simply putting passive for active, we derive as equivalent

    (iv) s is aware that something F is perceived by s .

Then, employing the sort of move involved in deriving (ii) from (i), we have as equivalent to (iv)

    (v) s is aware of something F as (*qua*) peceived by s.

The move from (iii) to (v) is exactly similar to that from 3 to 4. This line of argument will be open against any theory which treats perception as intentional or propositional and treats full consciousness as internal perception. If we regard awareness as an extensional relation no such development will be possible. If 'aware of ' is taken extensionally, from

    (vi) s is aware of something F

it does not follow that

    (vii) s is aware of something as F.

This is not to deny that (vii) or (ii) to which it is identical will not usually or perhaps invariably be true whenever (vi) is true: the transformation of acquaintance into knowledge, as the norm, is constitutive of human consciousness. But it does show that (vi) is not exhaustively analysed by (i) and (ii) (or (vii)) as Armstrong would say that it was.

If the Armstrongian theory leads to Berkeley's conclusion it is obviously self-refuting. If it is not to be self-refuting we must abandon either the view that introspection is a form of perception or the view that perception is essentially propositional. The only moves open would seem to be to adopt a straightforwardly behaviouristic account of either introspection and self-consciousness or of perception. But to reform the theory of perception would be very awkward, for a behaviourist theory of perception naturally carries with it a propositional one. For, on such an account, to perceive something F is to gain, through the senses, an F-appropriate disposition. But the possession of such a disposition is what it is, for a behaviourist, to have the belief that something F is present (see ch. 6.1). All the causal theorist can do is abandon his doctrine of introspection.

There is an important footnote to be added to these arguments against Armstrong's theory of consciousness. Argument (1) applies only to Armstrong's version of the theory according to which consciousness is interpreted in terms of one part of the brain scanning another part. But the general theory does not only have this physicalist or identity theory interpretation. It would be possible − though less likely − for a behaviourist or functionalist to interpret consciousness or self-consciousness in terms of one mental state directed on to another. In these cases, the mental states are abstract or constructed entities in some way grounded on brain states, but not identical with these physical states. Arguments (2) to (4) work quite generally against two-tier analyses of consciousness combined with a propositional account of awareness and do not depend upon the particular central state materialist interpretation that analysis receives on Armstrong's theory.

7 BEHAVIOURISM AND THE CAUSAL THEORY BACK TO SQUARE ONE

The important conclusion that we can draw is that, after criticism, the causal theory is much closer to classical behaviourism than its creators seem to intend. It survives only in the functionalist form and the only difference between functionalism and behaviourism is this: the behaviourist says that to be in a mental state is to be disposed to behave in some appropriate manner, whereas the causal theorist says that it is to be caused by something that is a part of oneself to be disposed to behave in this manner. He cannot, as he hoped, identify the disposition with the cause. Therefore, perception of the cause cannot count as perception of the disposition, and so it cannot count as consciousness or introspection of the disposition which is the mental state. Armstrong and a behaviourist could be in complete agreement as to what was going on in the world: their only difference concerns what of those goings-on are referred to by mental ascriptions. Armstrong's behaviourist takes 'disposition' in a purely phenomenalistic sense: he thinks that a categorical cause must underlie it and that there is such a cause is something to which we commit ourselves in ascribing mentality. This limited modification of behaviourism is an improvement but it does not remove the range of intuitive objections to behaviourism as Armstrong thinks that it does.

It is impossible to overemphasise two things. The first is that the behaviouristic (because dispositional) nature of the causal theory's analysis of mind prevents the identification of the mental state with the categorical structure of a part of the body. Second, this failure and the (connected) failure of his doctrine of introspection and consciousness prevent the causal theorist from developing that theory of current consciousness which would give his account real intuitive superiority over behaviourism.

Armstrong was well aware of how essential his doctrine of introspection was to him. He acknowledged that the mere postulation of an internal cause for behaviour does nothing to remove the counter-intuitiveness of behaviourism. He admits that, without some further account of introspection (which 'brain-scanning' is meant to provide), the causal theory is as viciously 'third person' as is behaviourism. Indeed the functionalist version of the causal theory which now remains is little different from behaviourism as often understood. A weak realism about dispositions is not alien to modern behaviourist thought.

Quine is normally regarded as a behaviourist, yet when discussing dispositions in *Word and Object* he says:

What we have seen dissolve in water had, according to the theory, a structure suited to dissolving; and when now we speak of some new dry sugar lump as soluble, we may be considered merely to be saying that it, whether destined for water or not, is similarly structured ... Dispositions are, we see, a better-behaved lot than the general run of subjunctive conditionals; and the reason is that they are conceived as built-in, enduring structural traits. (1960: 223)

When discussing the specifically mental characteristic of disposition to assent he says, 'The disposition may be presumed to be some subtle structural condition, like an allergy and like solubility; like an allergy, more particularly, in not being understood' (1960: 33-4). And in an unpublished Voice of America Forum Lecture (Philosophy of Science Series, no. 7) he says:

Intelligence today is where solubility was centuries ago. Still I think it is a promissory note. I do not think we would use the word 'intelligent' if we did not think there was an unidentified but some day identifiable causal agency or mechanism that sets one man above another in learning and in the solving of problems.

All this shows that Quine regards the ordinary notion of disposition as being realistic and involving topic neutral (at least when we are ignorant, if not after) reference to a structural state. Perhaps Armstrong concentrated too exclusively on Ryle and thereby came to an unbalanced assessment of modern behaviourism.

Another, much earlier, example of the adaptation of behaviourism so as to accommodate Armstrongian doctrines is found in a paper by Mace:

A reasonable behaviourist of the analytical type is, I believe, defensible subject to the following condition. First the concept of behaviour must be extended to cover not only bodily acts, but also bodily states, bodily dispositions, bodily 'states of readiness' to behave or act in various ways. The point of this reservation may be seen from the objection which Broad rightly points out to one sort of behaviourist analysis of perception. It is clear that when I perceive in one single glance many of the contents of a room there is no evidence that I am behaving (in any ordinary sense of the word) in regard to all the objects I perceive. It may, however, be said with some plausibility that, in perceiving any object, I am in a 'state of readiness' to behave in a way I should not be ready to behave in if I did not perceive it. And this 'adjustment' might be said to constitute the perception. The extension of the word 'behaviour' enables the behaviourist to deal with many psychological facts which otherwise might nonplus him. (1948-9: 4-5)

In this passage 'behaviour' is extended to cover all physical activity and states and a realist theory of dispositions is implicit (bodily dispositions, bodily 'states of readiness'). The rather ungenerous conclusion to which one is forced is that, without the doctrine of introspective consciousness, the causal theory is not novel, but is what one might call 'standard non-Rylean behaviourism'. When

77

discussing behaviourism we saw Broad shadowing the retreat into physicalism by those behaviourists who placed the burden of their theory on the notion of covert behaviour. Perhaps Armstrong misperceived his own stand by concentrating his opposition on those behaviourists who make much of the notion of disposition and, furthermore, just happen to have a non-realist theory of them. Given that his account of consciousness is a failure, Armstrong's theory and the causal theory in general collapse into this rather physicalistic behaviourism, which we have called 'functionalism'.

5

The disappearance theory

At the beginning of chapter 1 we referred to three types of materialist theory. The most dramatic-sounding of these, namely the theory that sensations and consciousness do not exist, has as yet barely been mentioned. In this brief chapter I shall discuss the so-called 'disappearance' or 'elimination' theory of mind. The purpose of that discussion is to show two things. The first is that the disappearance theory, must, if it is to be coherent, involve the causal or functionalist theory: it does not represent an alternative approach. The second is that those elements in the theory that go beyond this, and which might be deemed its original parts, are misleading and generally false.

The motive for propounding the disappearance theory was to avoid analytical reductionism. Such reductionism will, in Richard Rorty's opinion, 'inevitably get bogged down in controversy about the adequacy of proposed topic-neutral translations of statements about sensations' (1965-6: 27). He therefore suggests an alternative form of the identity theory which supposedly does not involve giving any analysis of psychological discourse. According to the proposed theory, mental and physical are not related by strict Leibnitzian identity, and therefore there is no necessity of claiming that everything that can truly be said of one can truly be said of the other. Instead, he chooses as the model for the relation between mental and physical states the relation of entities in a scientific theory which is about to be abandoned to those entities which are postulated in the theory which is replacing it, and which perform the same explanatory role as the entities in the original theory.

There is an obvious sense of 'same' in which what used to be called 'a quantity of calorific fluid' is *the same thing* as what is now called a certain mean kinetic energy of molecules but there is no reason to think that all features truly predicated of the one may be sensibly predicated of the other. The translation form of the theory holds that if we really understood what we were saying when we said things like 'I am having a stabbing pain' we should see that since we are talking about 'topic-neutral' matters we might, for all we know, be talking about brain processes. The disappearance form holds that it is unnecessary to show that suitable translations (into 'topic-neutral' language) of our talk about sensations can be given — as unnecessary as to show that statements about quantities of calorific fluid, when properly understood, may be seen as topic-neutral statements. (Rorty, 1965-6: 26-7)

This approach is not unique to Rorty but is common among philosophers of a pragmatist bent: in the course of this discussion we shall call upon the developments that Paul Feyerabend and Wilfrid Sellars make to the theory. As Rorty's examples show, he is forced to recognise three types of case which fall under his general scheme, according to which one postulated entity is replaced by another. First, there is the replacement of one entity known only by inference by another entity known only by inference. Second, there is the relegation of something which was taken to be an object of perception to the status of a merely phenomenal object. Third, there is the replacement of one directly or non-inferentially known entity by another directly known entity. The last type of case is the one relevant to the philosophy of mind, for the move in question in the debate on sensations is the claim that it is brain processes of which we are non-inferentially aware, not sensations. That reductive moves of the first two types are legitimate, is, presumably uncontroversial. The abandonment of one microscopic theory in favour of another (e.g. the theories of heat referred to by Rorty above) would be an instance of the first type. An instance of the second would be the discovery that certain putative visions were merely hallucinations, and that, therefore, the supposed entities which figured as the objects of the experience did not actually exist. The third differs from these two in that it involves claiming that the phenomenal contents of experience are other than they seem: it is one thing to postulate different explanations of the same evidence whilst accepting, in the barest observational terms, what that evidence is — for example, to accept that someone can see figures with horns and green faces, but tell him that they are not real, but only drug-induced and hallucinatory — and quite another to decide that the immediate observational content is of a wholly different nature from what had previously been thought. It is natural to think that what types of qualities figure as contents of experience cannot be a matter of dispute or revision (such a belief does not, of course, involve believing in the incorrigibility of any particular instance). Rorty is aware that the difference between the first two and the third case is that, in the former cases, we can 'save the phenomena' (1965-6: 37).

It is important to realise exactly how strange and counterintuitive Rorty's position is. Although pains are not such clearly delineated objects as patches of colour or tune images, nevertheless it seems clear to us that when we suffer a pain sensation a certain feature is present in our consciousness; the general nature of this feature and that it is present are both facts which standardly admit of no serious doubt. It is one thing to deny that our knowledge of our own mental states is incorrigible in any given case, and quite another to deny that we certainly know what types of 'feel' tend to occur in the content of such states. We can recognise pain sensations — we can say that the sensation we had today was like the one we had yesterday; that is, we are aware of something of a more or less determinate and recognisable nature. This is the experience of having a pain sensation. It is this pain sensation that Rorty is telling us does not exist: what we are non-inferentially aware of when we are 'in pain' is not such a sensation — it is a brain state. It is not being claimed that the brain state is the sensation, or that it possesses those qualities which we had previously taken to be possessed by the sensation; those features of which we thought we were aware are not properties of the brain state, but properties of something called a 'sensation', which, it has been decided, does not exist. Neither, then, do the features it was supposed to bear. The same applies to the features of visual or auditory sensations and images.

It must initially strike us as absurd to claim that we are wrong to believe that we are aware of a certain more or less determinate and recognisable feature when we suffer a pain or have a visual image. One natural reaction is to say that we could never have empirical or scientific reasons for doubting the existence of such things, for no evidence purporting to show that they do not exist could possibly be as clear and certain as the evidence we have from direct awareness that they do exist. Furthermore, as all our sensory information is mediated through sensation, if these sensations might be so radically misinterpreted as to be fictions, how much more precarious must be our theorising based upon them.

It is, therefore, not surprising that Rorty feels obliged to defend his claim that the third type of replacement is as legitimate as the first two. His defence is obscure, but it is the core of his thesis; if we grant him what he says here the rest is plausible. He defends himself by saying that the view that we have always in fact been referring non-inferentially to brain states by our sensation talk and not at all to sensation qualities

can hardly be rejected *a priori* unless we hold that we can only be taught to respond to the occurrence of As with the utterance 'A!' if we were able, prior to this teaching, to be aware, when A was present, that it was present. But this latter claim is plausible only if we assume that there is an activity which can reasonably be called 'awareness' prior to the learning of language. (1965-6: 40)

That there is not such pre-linguistic awareness might be thought to be a controversial thesis, and therefore one which required argument. But Rorty is not willing to oblige us: 'I do not wish to fight once again the battle which has been fought by Wittgenstein and many of his followers against such a notion of awareness. I wish rather to have taken it as having been won' (ibid.).

The view that there is something in our experience which is not constructed by the language or 'theory' with which we are operating is often referred to as the *doctrine of the given*. Intuitively, it might seem obvious that something in experience must be prior to our conceptualising; there must be something we get to work on. However, the given suffers from being closely associated with empiricism and hence is unfashionable. Too much has been written on this subject for me to deal with it here. I shall seek more limitedly to show that Rorty's application of modern scepticism about pre-linguistic awareness leads to ridiculous consequences.If this is favourable towards the given that will be a side benefit.

2 REFUTATION OF THE THEORY

The principal difficulty with Rorty's theory is simple and radical. If everything in our experience is subject to revision on theoretical grounds, why are we not able to revise our picture of the world until we have a world of our choosing? What is to stop us eliminating death, poverty and unhappiness by conceptual revisions? The role of the given was to fix the constraints within which theorising must take place; it presented the given facts which we must accommodate. But if there are no given facts, then why not adopt the theory which models the world on our desires?

We will make some remarks about this problem in general later. First, consider how it affects the philosophy of mind. At first sight

Rorty's proposed revision of the world is one which will make it a better place to live in. After his reforms there will be no sensations of pain (unfortunately, none of pleasure either). Out of charity, I shall assume that Rorty does not believe that his proposals have that consequence: I shall assume that he does not believe that, if we adopt his theory, breaking a limb will *ipso facto* become less nasty, unpleasant and painful than it was in the Cartesian world; he presumably does not think that these basic negative features of life are illusory in the way calorific fluid is. It seems that what he wants to abolish is the pain sensation, together with its experiential or mentalistic qualities, without abolishing pains, *in the sense that* the world is not supposed to become any less unpleasant, and people are not supposed to cease getting *hurt* and *suffering* as a result of this modification. At first sight this seems to be a straight contradiction, for the suffering and the hurting just *are* the qualities of a pain sensation. For illumination as to how a world without pain sensations is supposed to be an equally nasty world we must abandon Rorty, who has nothing to say on this matter, and turn to his ideological ally, Feyerabend. In his essay 'Materialism and the Mind–Body Problem' he argues that:

A new theory of pains will not change the pains; nor will it change the causal connections between the occurrence of pains and the production of 'I am in pain', except, perhaps very *slightly*. It will change the meaning of 'I am in pain.' Now it seems to me that observational terms should be correlated with causal antecedents, not with meanings. (1963-4: 58)

We are acquainted with types of word constancy following a similar model to that which Feyerabend wishes to impose on sensations. For example, if new discoveries about a creature lead us to reclassify it as a mammal instead of as a fish, our concept of what sort of thing that creature is will change, but its name will almost certainly remain the same, and so will the normal *prima facie* criteria for recognising a creature of that type. But the schema is not applicable to sensations, for it leaves out an essential element.

As Feyerabend's explanation is given above, it contains reference to four things: (1) the sentence 'I am in pain', (2) the meaning of that sentence, (3) the occurrence of the pain, which is the cause of the sentence's being uttered, and (4) the causal antecedents of the utterance (i.e. the stimulus) and the production of the utterance (i.e. the response to the stimulus). There seems to be something missing, namely (5) the experiencing of the pain, or the undergoing un-pleasantness: that aspect of the world which we have agreed the disappearance theorist cannot seriously be intending to abolish. One might presume that this is missing because it is held to be nothing over and above the occurrence of the pain, even though the pain is not a sensation, but only a brain process. According to mentalistic theories of pain, the occurrence of the pain and its being experienced may be taken as the same event, for it may be held that, for a pain, considered as a form of sensation, *esse est percipi*. But where the sensation (i.e. the mentalistic element) is being abolished and the pain is being identified with a brain process, of which the existence does not depend on its being experienced (not in the usual way, at least) one can ask what is that brain state's being experienced, over and above its occurring. There is nothing intrinsic about a brain process that can be identified with the *feeling* of a pain − 'hurting' is not a property of physical states, according to physical theory; thus we want to know what it is about this brain state which is its hurting. Because the hurting and the nastiness are aspects which are supposed to be common to the mentalistic and physicalistic concepts of pain, we can ask the question 'What was the *correct* element in the "pre-scientific" concept of pain?' The two questions 'What is it about the brain state which is its hurting?' and 'What was the correct element in the pre-scientific concept of pain?' are essentially the same question, for they ask for an account of the nastiness of pain which does not involve sensations or their qualities and which explains how the same phenomenon − namely the nastiness of the pain or what it is like to feel a pain − can be recognised as present when one is operat-ing with either a mentalistic or a physicalistic account of pain. That is to say, what is wanted is topic-neutral account of pain. Furthermore, in so far as Feyerabend gives any account of the element common to both theories, it is such a topic-neutral account. It is (4) which tells us what the ineliminable painfulness of the brain state consists in, namely its relation to a certain stimulus and a certain response. Thus a brain state is a pain, or the replacement for a pain, if and only if it is of a type caused by the appropriate stimulus and giving rise to the appropriate response. But this differs little from the causal or func-tional analysis of what we mean by 'pain'. If this pattern of explana-tion is to be applicable generally to mental predicates, then there must be some causal or functional account of what makes them predicable. The task of showing that there are such accounts, con-

84

cept by concept, is the task which the causal theorists have taken on and which disappearance theorists simply neglect.

3 HOW ITS MAIN EXPONENTS FAIL TO SEE THE PROBLEM

It is enlightening to compare the strategies of the 'analytic' and the 'disappearance' forms of the identity theory. The enlightenment will mainly come from contemplating the contrast between an approach which goes straight to the point, and another (not surprisingly, one with Hegelian roots) which mystifies the reader with talk of conceptual schemes and the development of theories, whilst hiding, barely discussed, those very problems that the first theory wrestles with in the full light of day.

The disappearance theory differs from the causal treatment of mental states in that it regards the advent of physicalism as part of an empirically based conceptual advance — one set of concepts or 'theory' is left behind and another replaces it: the meanings of terms retained from one to the next change. The causal analysis is not 'dynamic' in this way: the topic-neutral analysis is given as an exposition of the present notion of a mental state, which is not revised by physicalism. Sensations are particular types of mental state, not theoretical entities postulated in a primitive account of experience; they are not eliminated, but a correct analysis of them is provided. Furthermore, there is nothing in, say, *A Materialist Theory of the Mind* about concepts or meanings changing, let alone their passing away altogether. However, Armstrong (e.g. in ch. 12) and Smart (1963: 95) do deny the existence of purely phenomenal qualities, and in this sense they do advocate the rejection of something which had previously been admitted into our ontology. One can see the matter in this way: the causal theory says that there are no phenomenal qualities but there are sensations and these are in fact brain states with certain causal powers; the disappearance theory says that there are no phenomenal qualities and no sensations, but there are instead brain states with certain causal powers. This makes the difference appear trivial. But though the difference is trivial ontologically it is vital in the different foci of philosophical effort it entails. Because he claims that he can *analyse* talk of sensations in terms of things with a given causal role, the causal theorist is forced to face the question of what it is that makes a brain state adequate to the data of, or taking over the role of, experience. The very general scientific methodological considerations that motivate the dis-

85

appearance theory, on the other hand, do not press its protagonists into explaining closely how the job done by particular types of mental state can be taken over by physical processes. Indeed, we have seen that disappearance theorists let this obligation ride so lightly on their shoulders that they seem oblivious of the essential similarity of their account to the causal theory.

Wilkes has set the disappearance theory in its proper place. After presenting her functionalist analysis of the mental she applies 'disappearance' tactics to what is left over; that is, to those Cartesian elements which resist functional treatment (1978: 86-113). These bits of philosophico-scientific detritus are supposedly the remnants of a specifically Cartesian theory about the causes of behaviour. Wilkes is under no illusion that the disappearance theory represents an alternative strategy to reductive analysis. Nor, I think, would she say that it treats appropriately the pre-philosophical elements in our concept of experience; functionalism does that. The disappearance theory applies only to elements insinuated by Cartesianism.

4 A WORLD WITHOUT TABLES

There is one aspect of the Rorty—Feyerabend strategy which is particularly peculiar. We can all agree that as scientific theory develops entities like calorific fluid or demons might be dropped. And even if the elimination of sensations seems bizarre, the point of the claim that science might require that they be abandoned is fairly clear. But among the entities which Rorty and Feyerabend want to eliminate in their on-going purge of reactionary ontologies are ordinary macroscopic objects. Tables, chairs and lamp standards are as much the victims of their permanent revolution as are Cartesian souls. The only entities we should subscribe to are those in the most advanced scientific theory. It is only a matter of convenience that we retain discourse about anything else.

Rorty attacks the belief that 'the identity of tables with clouds of molecules does not permit us to infer the non-existence of tables' (1965-6: 33-4). All that stops us from abandoning the notion 'table' is that it would be 'monstrously inconvenient to do so' (ibid.). As far as I can tell, this inconvenience rests only on the commonness of the word 'table', and thus the amount of retraining of people that would be required. 'Nothing would be lost by the dropping of "table" from our vocabulary' because 'we could stop making a referring use of "table" and of any extensionally equivalent term, and still leave our ability to describe and predict undiminished' (ibid.). There is implicit here. an inadequate view of the uses of language: it would be sufficient only if language existed merely to give a catalogue of the basic entities in the world, from which all others are constructed. But I am usually interested in tables as tables, and they may vary enormously and arbitrarily in their properties as clouds of molecules whilst still being quite straightforward and similar as tables. How large a disjunct of possible types of clouds of molecules of all the materials from which tables can be made would give the same extension as 'table'? And if such a linguistic monster were bred, what element need the diverse clouds of molecules have in common except that they composed something recognisable and usable as a table? So while we are interested in tables as such the concept will survive, even if, *per impossibile*, it becomes the meaning of another term in scientific use (e.g. 'cloud-of-such-and-such-a-sort'). But why make a scientific description ambiguous in this way? To avoid ambiguity we would have to be prepared to reject objects that were plainly tables by their shape and use because they had unusual structures, or we would have to have an incomplete concept of the type of cloud in question to allow for new cases that intuition demanded we admit. Although we might not always be interested in tables (though it will always be true to say 'There were tables') we will always be interested in macroscopic objects which will differ from each other microscopically within each type, and thus macroscopic concepts are theoretically ineliminable. To make an analogy between dropping the concept 'table' and dropping the concept 'demon' when we decide that visions are mere hallucinations is misleading. Rorty suggests that we can say that there are no demons because it is not inconvenient to drop the concept 'demon' as a referring expression. But this misses the main difference between the two cases: demons were thought to be mind-independent entities, whereas they turned out in fact (according to Rorty's example, that is) to be mind-dependent images; thus demons as previously conceived did not exist. Tables, on the other hand, were thought to be independent physical objects, and they are just that: it is true that tables are made of some things not themselves tables, but no-one ever thought that tables were not made of smaller types of things: that tables are not ontologically basic can hardly count as a scientific discovery. It is worth noting that if Rorty were correct, not only such emotionally neutral objects as tables would come under the hammer. We should have to say that, strictly, there are no people – not even any human bodies. I do not even exist myself and only use 'I' because it would be 'monstrously inconvenient' to refer individually to all the particles that make me up. 'Particles' is presumably the correct term, for why should molecules escape? If the programme of a unified science can be carried through only the ménagerie of sub-atomic particles really exists.

It should be obvious that this 'translation out' of macroscopic terms is not a necessary adjunct of the disappearance form of the identity theory. For we are quite happy to say that tables are nothing more than collections of atoms whilst accepting that the concept 'table' has an irreplaceable function: thus attempts to make this concept disappear are irrelevant to materialism. The case where one object is replaced by another, as calorific fluid was replaced by molecules and their energy, is clearly a very different sort of case from that where an object – an x – is shown to consist of smaller objects not themselves xs.

Sellars (1965), claims to present a more reasonable theory about the durability and replaceability of the common-sense conception of the world. He is as many times more subtle than Feyerabend as he is more obscure, and criticises the latter for making the abolition of the common-sense framework prematurely. But his position is not really an improvement on Feyerabend's or Rorty's. Common sense he says, has a 'methodological primacy'. 'It is the rock bottom concepts and principles of common sense which are binding until a total structure which can do the job better is at hand' (1965: 189); or perhaps more important,

Only when the conceptual space of sense impressions has acquired a status which is not parasitical on the framework of common sense physical objects – in other words, only with the development of an adequate scientific theory of the sensory capacities of the central nervous system – could the framework of common sense be abandoned without losing conceptual contact with a key dimension of the world. (1965: 193)

The argument contained here is that, as our present sense-impression language is logically parasitic upon macroscopic physical-object language, and as human sense experience is a vital aspect of the world, macroscopic physical-object language cannot be abandoned until there is a new physicalist sensation language. However, Feyerabend argues that the choice between ordinary language and physicalist language for describing sensations can only be made when there is a 'fully developed materialistic idiom', and that 'materialese' must be allowed *at least* as much time to reach an adequate sophistication as it has taken ordinary English to develop (1963-4: 55). Thus Sellars's supposedly more subtle and restrained view is really as adventurous as Feyerabend's; the heavy Kantian moderation in his language is misleading.

As we do not naturally or intuitively think that accepting the reality of macroscopic objects challenges either materialism or science, why do Rorty, Feyerabend and Sellars think that it does? Presumably they think as follows. Concepts not denoting things in the basic scientific theory cannot figure in statements of what ultimately exists; therefore one either eliminates the things such concepts denote, as with demons or phlogiston, or one interprets the concept as denoting some object composed from entities in the basic theory, treating the concept as eliminable shorthand. But the second option involves a misunderstanding. If one eschews the simple elimination accorded phlogiston one is obliged to admit that the concept in question *denotes* things that are in fact composed of entities in the basic theory, but not that it connotes them as so composed. That is, there is no obligation to be able to *define*, for example, 'table' in terms of basic science. This is because the correctness of any particular specialised physical theory is not built into our ordinary concepts; they are topic neutral with regard to basic structure. Therefore, no particular microscopic physical description is a necessary condition for the satisfaction of a macroscopic concept and inter-definition is not possible. But some physical characterisation or open set of characterisations in the correct basic science must each be sufficient for the satisfaction of the concept, for there must be some basic structure descriptions which entail the macroscopic features in terms of which the concepts are defined (see ch. 2.4). This explains why a concept such as 'table' need not figure in a basic ontological catalogue and yet it not matter if it cannot be eliminated from our discourse. Ontologically it is redundant because there are not both table-like micro-structures and tables; conceptually it is not, because when we say there are tables we do not mean to be committing ourselves to a given scientific theory nor to denying that in a possible world made from different basic elements than ours there could be tables, for tables are not natural kinds. Materialism is in no way compromised by this relaxation of Rorty's rigour, for the requirement that non-eliminable concepts denote things formed only from approved structures preserves the ontological requirement.

5 THE LIMITS OF CONCEPTUAL RELATIVISM

Although we have been directly concerned mainly with the replaceability of mental entities, our discussion in this chapter raises general problems for the conceptual relativist. The relativist faces the difficulty of giving content to the assertion that theories A and B in some sense explain the same part of the world whilst also denying that there is anything which is given prior to them both, relative to which their common ground might be identified. The difficulty, then, is that if nothing is given pre-theoretically there would appear to be no grounds for claiming that any two theories concerned the same subject matter. The relativist might try the following way round the problem:

I agree that there is an important sense in which one cannot change the world by changing one's theory about it: this must be so if, for example, the world cannot be made more pleasant by abolishing talk of pain. But my assertion is not that the world is determined by our thought, only that no characterisation of the world can be made which is independent of the theory from within which it is made. The position is, therefore, not so much that there is no given as that there is no way of characterising that given in its own right – independently, that is, of a general theoretical viewpoint.

I do not believe that this position – that there is in a sense a given world but that one cannot say pre-theoretically what it is – is a coherent one. The reason is as follows. If we are to say that two theories A and B have, extensionally, the same ultimate subject matter, then there must be some possible ground for that claim. The only possible ground is that we can show or describe some of the facts or phenomena that they both purport to explain. But in so far as one can isolate this common element one could in principle introduce a vocabulary to characterise these elements and this vocabulary could be regarded either as a part of both theories or as a metadescription of a higher order than either.

I suspect that the relativist would deny this because he believes, like the absolute idealist, that every aspect of a language or theory is, in some way, 'infected' by the presence of the rest of the language or theory of which it is a part. Therefore, although one can perhaps ostensively show what subject matter the two have in common, as

90

soon as we try to say as well as show what that is, even if we introduce a neutral, ostensively defined vocabulary to speak of what is shown, that vocabulary will become infected by the rest of our discourse. This claim may be backed up with comments about the secondary status of ostensively defined terms and how they can operate only within the context of a wider theory and not in their own right, So the suggestion above about a meta-vocabulary would not work, for one could not have a meta-language which was simply ostensive in its foundations and if it were incorporated into both A and B it would take on different senses in these contexts.

However, although one can identify the common element, it is not plausible to say that one cannot characterise it in a neutral fashion. For if I characterise a putatively common element in terms of theory A, then someone may ask how much of my A-theoretical characterisation a B-theorist would accept. If I can answer this question then I have provided a theory-neutral characterisation. If I cannot, then there is a problem, for if I refuse to identify the area of overlap between my characterisation and that of a B-theorist of the same phenomena, we are back in the position of having no reason for saying that we are both talking about the same phenomena. Simply put, the argument is this. If one can avoid the conclusion that we can change the world by thinking on it, we must agree that there is something pre-theoretical, namely the empirical world itself. And if we are to be able to say rationally that two theories cover the same part of the world, we must be able to identify that in a way intelligible from the standpoint of both theories. And if we can show what is common, so that people can recognise it as the common element, then we can have a name or description which picks it out as just that: for, on no sensible theory could one be able to *see that* it is common without being able to say *what* is common. What can be recognised as such and such can *eo ipso* be named as such and such. Therefore, I can see no plausibility in the claim that ostensively definable elements common to two theories must differ in their senses because of their association with the rest of the theory. That they do so differ does not follow from the weaker thesis that ostension is only possible within some sort of framework or language which is itself a going concern: that is, it does not follow from the thesis that one cannot have a purely ostensive language or a language somehow constructed from or resting on ostensive elements.

Loose use of such terms as 'grammar', 'logical form' or 'concep-

91

tual scheme' must not be allowed to lead us into confusing two claims. One claim might be called 'the holism of logic or grammar'. This asserts that such categories of activity as naming, ostension and describing are what they are because of their position in an overall structure of grammatical or logical functions and that, therefore, without the total structure there could be no such functions and that a different structure without these functions would provide no definite mapping for them. The other claim might be called 'the holism of empirical content'. This asserts that substantial elements within two theories, differing in their substantial postulates but not in their basic grammars, depend for their sense on their relation to the other substantial elements in the theory. On the first theory, naming, for example, will be what it is because of its relation to other linguistic activities. On the second, if taken in the entirely general way that relativism requires, 'red', for example, will mean something quite different in a theory which contains knowledge about light waves from one which does not. Even if one were to deny that there is the absolute distinction between form and content that my distinction seems to imply, it remains the case that most, at least, of the so-called' 'conceptual revisions' demanded by science are of the second sort and do not overthrow basic logical and grammatical categories.

The 'holism of empirical content' must not be confused with the innocuous claim that ostended concepts will tend to acquire accretions of meaning from their association with other elements in a theory, for it concerns rather whether they can in principle be stripped of such accretions in a way that enables them to be theory neutral. No doubt, for example, 'red' now has associations with theories about light waves, but it can easily be stripped of these and referred back to the *look* of things when philosophical or other purposes require. The innocent holism which asserts that terms do get infected must not be turned into the holistic superstition that they must be and must remain so infected.

Perhaps it will be said that what I have proved so far is of minimal interest. I have shown only that, for any two theories which purport to cover the same material, there must be some element common to them both. But this is not to prove the 'given' in the traditional sense, for that asserts that there must be something common and prior to all theories that cover the same ground. Clearly, the latter does not follow from the former: for if there are three theories A, B and C, A and B may have feature-group F in common, B and C may have G in common and A and C have H in common, although there is nothing that A, B and C have in common. Therefore, I must argue that this situation cannot arise. And indeed it cannot, for the following reason. A and B are required to possess some feature in common for them to count as theories about the same thing. But in key cases, such as that where A is the traditional theory of mind, there is a further constraint, namely that *certain features* of A be preserved. This has been clear all along from our insistence that it is *the nastiness* of pain that must not be lost. If this is the case − namely that there are respects in which we are not prepared to accept that conceptual reform could reform the actual world − then any theory that succeeds A, or succeeds a successor of A, must preserve this element. The case of overlapping theories, with no one element common to all but elements common to predecessor and successor, cannot apply in this case. Such a reform could clearly take place in the realm of the purely theoretical and, by the element of overlap, give pragmatically adequate sense to the claim that contiguous theories possessed the same subject matter, though this could hardly be said of theories more distant along the chain. What justifies and forces us to acknowledge the fundamentality of a distinction between the empirical (or sensory, or phenomenal) and the theoretical is the fact that certain features of the world cannot be revised away by purely conceptual techniques: not merely can nastiness not be abolished by one conceptual revision, a whole series could not remove it. And for this to make sense, at each stage we must be able to identify what is being preserved as what we now call the nastiness in the world, and similar considerations apply as did when we were discussing only two theories. The ineliminable is not the preserve of the mental. No adequate theory could allow that a man jumping from a window does not fall, nor could it lack means of expressing this in a way manifestly translatable into ours. The area of unrevisable fact is quite broad.

To be sure, Feyerabend does elsewhere deny this last statement. He implies, for example, that our belief that if we jumped out of an upstairs window we would fall is an entirely theory-bound belief: our belief that any theory which says otherwise is, in some objective sense, false is a piece of pure superstition (1975: 221-2). But such extreme epistemological anarchism is not something that many people would want to accept. It does suggest that, by conceptual or theoretical adjustment, we could abolish the nastiness of pain or indeed anything else. If we choose a theory that says all Frenchmen are really illusions, or says that whenever we thought we had a plate of roast beef we really have a glass of claret, then there is no objective standard by which such a theory is false. Against this very general epistemological radicalism I cannot argue here, for it would require an essay of its own to refute it by any more rigorous method than pointing out its outrageousness. That it is outrageous is plain, and for our purposes we shall treat the need for the disappearance theory or the attack on the given to adopt such a position as a *reductio ad absurdam*.

6

Reductive theories of perception

I PERCEPTION, BELIEF AND BEHAVIOUR

We have whittled the materialist options down to one, namely behaviourism with a realist theory of dispositions. This theory is functionalism. It does not suffer from behaviourism's inability to state the necessary and sufficient conditions for being in a given mental state, for statements of the form 's is in mental state M if and only if there is some state internal to s which grounds (or realises) his disposition to M-behave' do state at least a plausible extensional equivalence. But the behaviourist's inability to cope with subjectivity or consciousness remains unremedied. In that sense, functionalism is just as counterintuitive as behaviourism. In this chapter I hope to improve on intuition by presenting an argument to show that all behaviouristic theories of perception are false. The argument works against traditional functionalism and the causal theory, and is essentially independent of the arguments employed in previous chapters.

A behaviouristic approach to perception is sometimes explicity married to a belief theory of perception (e.g. in Armstrong, 1968, chs. 10 and 11; Pitcher, 1971). In this case, perception is subjected to a two fold reduction. First, perceiving an object is analysed as no more than acquiring, in some appropriately immediate way, the belief that the object is present. Second, the possession of that belief is explained as no more than the possessing of a capacity to behave in the appropriate discriminatory way with respect to that object. The integration of the belief theory into the behaviouristic approach is, from the viewpoint of the latter, not merely natural but necessary. For the possession of a certain behavioural readiness (or of a state enshrining such a readiness) will be what it is to possess a belief, if the behaviour in question is of the appropriate sort. The resources of the theories in question force one, after making allowance for the other desires and the desires that form part of one's holistic interpretation of the person's psychology, to equate *believing that p* and *being set up to behave as if p were true*. Therefore, if perceiving an object is equivalent

95

to acquiring a disposition to behave as if that object were present, it must also be equivalent to acquiring a belief that that object is present: thus the behaviouristic theories entail the belief theory. Someone who believes that the possession of a belief necessarily involves the possession of verbal capacities might deny this, for perceptual dispositions can be acquired by creatures lacking language. However, this refinement is irrelevant for the purposes of discussing human perception. We can assume that humans do have a linguistic capacity and, in that context, an appropriate behavioural disposition must count as a belief. The appropriate disposition is not, of course, simply a linguistic one. It is one thing to say that only creatures with language have beliefs and another to say that a belief consists simply in a linguistic disposition. The most that could be required is that, together with the other dispositions, one have the *capacity* to put the belief into words.

On the other hand, there is no entailment between the belief theory of perception and a behaviouristic theory of belief: it is logically possible to hold the former with a non-reductive, mentalistic account of belief. However, I am not aware of anyone who does; in practice the only motive for holding the belief theory is the belief that it is the first move in a materialist account of consciousness.

Because behaviouristic theories of perception entail the belief theory, it would be possible to refute the former by refuting the latter. In order to do this we must first establish the Principle of Minimal Empiricism.

2 THE PRINCIPLE OF MINIMAL EMPIRICISM

The Principle of Minimal Empiricism (PME) can be expressed as follows. As a matter of fact, the ability of humans to conceive of the empirical world depends on their possessing senses through which they can experience that world. Some of their concepts must be definable or 'cashable' or (as I shall usually say) demonstrable with reference to some quality as that quality is presented in experience: that is, some qualities must be able to figure as objects of experience such that subjects are able to recognise and discrimate them. It is not necessary that any particular concepts are those that should be so demonstrable, or that the identity of the conceptual scheme between persons depends on their having the same experientially demonstrable ones − I am not, for example, ruling out the possibility that people with different senses may, if they develop similar theories, be said to have the same conception of the world. This principle is well summarised by Feigl:

> Our world, being what it is, can, of course, be known by description in any of its parts or aspects, but only on the basis of a foothold somewhere in acquaintance. This, it seems to me, is one of the cornerstones of any empiricist epistemology old or new. But the new empiricism of recent times has come to recognize that it matters little just which areas of acquaintance are available or actually utilized ... the congenitally blind deaf person ... could in principle construct and confirm a complete system of the natural science. (1958: 433)

Perhaps a stronger version of empiricism could be justified, but this very weak form is all that my argument will require. A similar doctrine can be found in Quine when he talks of knowledge as 'a man-made fabric which impinges on experience only at the edges' (1953: 42). The fact that 'our statements about the external world face the tribunal of sense experience not individually but only as a corporate body' (1953: 41), makes no difference to the essential point. Even if the demonstrable elements in language cannot exist without the rest of language, it is still true that language as a whole is empirically interpreted only in so far as some elements are demonstrable. If discourse 'impinges on experience' anywhere at all, the concepts employed at those places will be demonstrable. Anyone tempted to go further than Quine and sever the link between language and the world entirely by denying PME should consider the unacceptable consequences of such a move (see ch. 5.5). Suppose that the intelligibility of our empirical predicates does not rest upon the fact that some of them are empirically demonstrable: suppose, that is, that experience and language need never meet at any point for language to acquire empirical content. It follows either that language acquires content from connexion with something other than experience, or that it acquires content from its own coherence − that is, without reference to its relation to anything beyond itself. The first possibility has no intuitive plausibility for there seems to be nothing else with which it might appropriately be connected. Connexion with physical but unexperienced features will not suffice, for language is meaningful *to people* and such significance cannot stem solely from some speaker-independent relation. If, therefore, it is denied that connexion with demonstrable features of the world is essential, then one is saying that language has empirical content solely from its own structure − from the interrelation of terms within it. This is the claim that language can have empirical content while being a sort of uninterpreted calculus, a set of signs whose sense is fixed only by rules relating them to each other. I assume that it is a refutation of this view to point out that it leaves no convincing way of distinguishing empirical language and concepts from purely formal ones – that is, from an uninterpreted calculus. If this absurdity is rejected, then some predicates must be demonstrable and, therefore, PME is correct.

We must avoid a possible misunderstanding. It might at first be thought that PME directly rules out and therefore begs the question against behaviouristic theories by importing the notion, alien to behaviourism, of ostensive definition. However, given a behaviourist theory of perception, there is no incompatibility here. The empirical interpretation of our conceiving will consist in our ability to exhibit basic types of discriminatory behaviour in the face of basic macroscopic empirical features or objects. It will remain true that understanding of more abstract empirical concepts rests on our understanding of these and that demonstration of a concept will consist in the acquisition or reinforcing of these capacities for discrimination by being perceptually faced with the qualities to which the behavioural capacities relate. Such basic discriminatory behaviour will count as perception for the behaviourist – to be able to respond in a discriminatory way in the face of objects is to perceive them.

In summary, PME asserts two things. First, a capacity for experience akin to sense experience is a necessary condition for someone's being able to operate with language or concepts which are empirically interpreted. Second, sense experience facilitates this interpretation because sensible features and qualities demonstrably feature as its objects, such that the sentient creature can recognise or discriminate these features.

3 PERCEPTION, CLAIRVOYANCE AND THE 'DENSITY THEORY'

One way of attacking the belief theory is to deny that we are always cognitively moved when we have a sense experience. It has, for instance, been argued that for the most part after-images do not give rise in one to any tendency to believe that an object is present. I shall not be following this line of objection, for though the statement that not all experience is accompanied by some form of belief may be true, it is not demonstrably so if one takes into account Armstrong's subtle apparatus of tendencies to believe and potential belief (1968:

223f). My strategy is to argue that, whether or not all experience is accompanied by some mode of belief, it cannot consist solely in that, for if it did there could be no grounds for ascribing to experience the unique role PME assigns to it.

At its simplest, the problem for the belief theory is to explain how to distinguish experience from other forms of belief acquisition, for it is obvious that not every acquisition of a belief about some thing is also a seeming perception of that thing. For example, if A tells B about the cup final it does not seem to B that he perceives the cup final, although he acquires beliefs about it. This point is isolated in a useful way in the difference between the following cases:

(1) s looks at and sees an orange patch on the wall.
(2) While facing the wall with his eyes closed there comes to s the true belief that there is an orange patch on the wall, although it does not seem to s that he experiences it visually.

It is at least logically possible that there should be a clairvoyant ability of the sort described in (2). As both (1) and (2) involve the involuntary acquisition of belief about a particular feature of the environment, what constitutes the difference between them such that (1) presents itself as a sense experience and (2) does not? Let us call the special phenomenal or experiential element present in (1) 'P', and consider various accounts of it that have been, or might be offered. The first suggestion would be that P is the property of being acquired through the senses; that is, via some sense organ. Armstrong regards the role of the sense organs in a somewhat equivocal way, finally deciding that reference to them is 'helpful but has not a full right to appear in the definition' (1968: 212). The inadequacy of invoking the senses to analyse P is shown by the following consideration.

It will not suffice to distinguish (1) from (2) simply on the grounds that the belief in (1) comes via a sense organ, for it can be no more than a contingent truth that clairvoyant revelations as in (2) do not come through some organ. Indeed, if there were ever to be a physical explanation of clairvoyance it might involve identifying some brain area as a receptor for the information. Nor will it do to say that this organ of clairvoyance would not be a *sense* organ, on the grounds that it does not provide real experience, for that will merely make it necessary for us to define experience proper before we can identify sense organs, as against other information-gathering organs, whereas the proposal under present consideration is precisely to move in the opposite direction by citing the presence of sense organs as a criterion for experience. Someone who wishes to distinguish (1) from (2) solely on the grounds that (1) involves an organ is committed to the view that we can know *a priori* that clairvoyance has no organ and such a commitment seems absurd.

A more promising approach to P is provided by Pitcher (1971: 70-1).[1] He adopts what I shall call the 'density theory' of P. According to the density theory the special nature of experience is a function of the great number of beliefs that are acquired therein. Thus, when s perceives an orange patch on the wall, he is not merely being stimulated to the single vague belief that there is an orange patch on the wall, but is receiving information relating to every minimally discriminable point in his visual field: his phenomenal picture is built up from those minute pieces of information like a newspaper photograph from dots. The same object of awareness, therefore, is repeatedly presented both spatially and temporally to build up an enduring extended visual patch.

To illuminate the density theory let us introduce some simple terminology and make a warning remark. Let us call the general or large scale belief shared by both perceiver and clairvoyant a 'macro-belief' and the beliefs that go to make up the macro-belief of the perceiver but which are absent in the case of the clairvoyant 'micro-beliefs'. These correspond to the minimal discriminations of which the subject is capable. As we are agreed, a macro-belief which is constructed from micro-beliefs is introspectively different from one which is not so constructed: to agree to this is merely to agree, as does Pitcher, that perceptual experience has some quality not possessed by the adventitious arrival of a belief. The warning is that it must be noticed that this difference is *constituted by* and not *caused by* the density of micro-beliefs. If it were merely a matter of causation then the resulting experiential feel would not be analysed by the density theory, but only causally explained by it and it would remain an unanalysed phenomenon.

The density theory has some intuitive appeal, for richness of informational content certainly is a feature of experience. However, I propose to show that it cannot be used to provide an analysis of P.

We have so far argued that sense experiences reveal the nature of their objects in a way in which other non-sensory mental activities do not; and that they differ from other such activities by a feature we

---

1   Armstrong expressed similar views in discussion at a seminar given by D. Cooper and M. Sainsbury in Oxford, 1969.

have called 'P' which corresponds to their experiential or phenomenal feel. Intuition suggests that we should put these two points together, and conclude that it is in virtue of P — the experiential feel of sensing — that it is able to deliver up its object in the special and revealing way. In other words, the clairvoyant, whose experience lacks P, would not be in a position to grasp a new quality by that manner of experience in the sort of way someone could become acquainted by normal perception with some quality new to him. Unless some completely different mode of comprehension is involved (and that is of no account to the present case) a clairvoyant could not learn the look of a new colour by this type of experience. It follows that if P is the same thing as belief density, it is belief density which satisfies the PME by revealing the nature of sensible qualities.

But how can this be so? According to the density theory, P is no more than the repetition of the same type of mental act, namely the acquisition of an ordinary belief. The information that x is red, when presented densely is more extensive in spatio-temporal coverage than when presented as a single belief, but what is presented, namely the property in the predicate position in the description of the belief, is exactly the same. If such repetition produced a difference in the nature of the internal object of the act, this could only be an emergent feature of the situation. Though it might, in some sense, supervene upon the density of the information, the essentially different nature of the presence of the same content could not be analysed in terms of sheer repetition. To claim so would be to employ the 'ignorant foreigner' principle: if you shout it loud and often enough he will come to understand.

In general, it is difficult to see how the belief theorist can accommodate P using only the materials he permits himself. If P really affects the internal object of the act it would seem that it could do so only in one of two ways. It might affect the way the predicative element or object figures in the act, so that the type of internal object that figures in s sensing red is different from that which figures in s believing that something is red. But then, for the reasons just given, it appears impossible that the former should be reductively analysed in terms of the latter. Extent of information can never amount to a difference within the very same predicative property that is present in each piece of information. (I am not, of course, disputing that further things may be inferred from a great mass of information — e.g. that from a mass of information that a set of points are red one might infer the shape of a red thing — but only that sheer volume of information of the type 'red at p' can tell you more about the nature of red.)

The other option is to say that when P is present the predicative content itself is different, so that for any predicate F, if F can be sensed it cannot be thought etc. This is manifest nonsense.

The rationale of this objection can perhaps be generalised and defended in the following argument. The first premise is a general statement of PME:

(1) It is a necessary condition for anyone's having the ability to comprehend objects of cognitive activity which concerns the empirical world that he be able to grasp (recognise, demonstrate etc.) some objects of sensory activity.

The second is a statement of the density theory:

(2) The objects of sensory acts are logical constructions from those of cognitive acts: e.g. seeming to see something red is to be analysed as having beliefs (in a certain manner) about the presence of something red.

The third is a general principle about the relation of constructions or analysanda to their elements or analysantia:

(3) If As are logical constructions from Bs then it cannot be logically necessary that someone comprehend As as a requirement for his comprehending Bs.

Therefore

(4) It cannot be logically necessary that someone comprehend the objects of sensory acts as a requirement for comprehending the objects of cognitive acts. ((2) (3), by substitution.)

But

(5), (1) and (4) are contradictories.

Therefore

(6) Given the truth of PME (i.e. of (1)) and the general theory of constructions, (3), the density theory (i.e. (2)) is false.

A possible line of defence against the argument centres on (3) and (4). Someone might deny that it is *logically* necessary that we grasp the objects of perceptual beliefs prior to grasping those of other beliefs, including the micro-beliefs that make up perceptual beliefs. Perhaps it is just a contingent fact that micro-beliefs fall below the threshold of consciousness; that is, it is contingent that we cannot notice them individually and therefore could not demonstrate our concepts by reference to them. Perhaps this is what Pitcher means when he makes the apparently bizarre claim that our conscious experience is made up of beliefs which are themselves 'one and all non-conscious' (1971: 71). This approach is easier to understand if one thinks of belief in a purely behaviouristic way. Thus the minimal pieces of information – construed as capacities for response – which we receive are subliminal; that is, they are too microscopic for us to be able to notice or report on them. The latter fact, however, is purely contingent. It could have been the case that we were able to monitor and report on the slightest of our information-induced behavioural modifications; but it is not. It now ceases to be logically necessary that we have macro-perceptual beliefs prior to comprehending others.

As it stands, this argument is not quite to the point. It does not prove that perceptual beliefs need not have been prior to others; it proves only that the micro-beliefs from which our macro-perceptual beliefs are constructed might themselves have been fully perceptual – that is, might have possessed P. If this were so then there would, clearly be no trouble about how macro-perceptual beliefs come to possess P, for the beliefs from which they are constructed also possess it. This would not solve the mystery of P, for the clairvoyant's belief does not possess it; neither do our ordinary non-perceptual beliefs.

However, an account of P is implicit in the above. It is that P is the feature of being noticeable; that is, it is the feature of being reportable. This account is typically behaviouristic in its form of reduction. But it still fails to distinguish the clairvoyant from the perceiver, for both can report on their beliefs. The next move is to argue that the clairvoyant's belief is too bare, too lacking in informational density. We are now in danger of moving in a circle, for we are back to the density explanation of P. The situation is as follows. We cannot allow the most minute micro-beliefs to possess P because although that would explain why macro-perceptual beliefs possess P it would not explain P itself, which is lacking in non-perceptual beliefs. Therefore let us assume that micro-perceptual beliefs and non-perceptual beliefs both lack P. Then the problem is how to analyse P. We have proved that it cannot be a logical construct from (and therefore a *necessary* consequence of) the density of beliefs which individually lack it. If P *contingently* arises from density, then it appears to be an emergent phenomenon over and above the belief, which is contrary to the belief theory of perception. We can avoid this by saying that it

103

is merely an emergent *capacity to* report one's beliefs, but then we fail to distinguish perception from clairvoyance. There is thus no way of explaining P by density of information while associating it also with PME, that is, with our ability to demonstrate and learn concepts via perception. We could, therefore, try dissociating P from PME and denying that it has anything to do with the revelatory role of perception. But this would take us no nearer to an account of what P is. The denial that it is connected with the seeming presence of the object deprives us of a lead, but does not suggest any answers other than those already discredited. There is one possibility, namely that P consists in the belief that one is getting an enormous number of beliefs relating to one compact area, corresponding to a sense field. In this case P just is a belief about perceptual beliefs, not a feature of them.

This approach looks hopeful from a behaviouristic point of view. This optimism can be dissipated by referring back to our discussion of Armstrong's theory of introspection. The theory of P being suggested is in fact a version of that account of introspection; for it is being suggested that normal perceptual consciousness (which is characterised by P) involves perceiving (acquiring beliefs about) one's perceptual beliefs. Arguments (2), (3) and (4) which we employed against Armstrong in chapter 4.6, and which we observed at the time would be equally efficacious against more purely behaviouristic theories of introspection, apply here. The common core to those arguments was that it is obviously false that the acquisition of full perceptual consciousness consists in a new awareness of one's own dispositions rather than a changed awareness of the original object of perception.

We can, therefore, conclude that the belief theory cannot cope with the phenomenon of perceptual experience. As we have already shown that any behaviouristic theory is committed to the belief theory, then behaviouristic theories, including functionalism, are refuted. When we introduced the problem of materialism and consciousness in chapter 1 we said that the behaviourist attempted to treat that component in subjectivity which challenges materialism, namely the 'what it is like' of perception, as nothing more than acquiring a disposition. He denies, that is, the presence of any internal object of awareness in the normal sense. The behaviourist claimed that what was lacked by the deaf scientist who knew everything about the physiology of hearing was merely the capacity for responding spontaneously to sounds, and not some information about the nature or quality of a subjective state. If our arguement is correct, information about the objects of consciousness would be lacking to the behaviourist and the dispositional treatment of experience is inadequate to its role of revealing the empirical world to us.

4 BEHAVIOURISM AND RECOGNITION

There is a valuable extension of the above argument against behaviouristic theories of perception, for it can be adapted for use against behaviouristic theories of conceptual activity. Such theories are more common then behaviourist theories of perception and have been popular with reductive empiricists who are content with the irreducibility of sense contents. For example, Ayer attempts to develop some ideas of this sort that he finds in Peirce (1968: 173-9). Any form of logical atomism or Humean theory of mind will be obliged to analyse the intensionality − that is, the significance − of mental contents in a behaviouristic manner. I shall argue that recognition of objects of awareness − that is, bringing them under concepts − cannot be given a behavioural analysis unless perceptual awareness itself can be so analysed. We have already shown that the latter cannot be so analysed; therefore, neither can recognition. But if recognition is not susceptible to behaviourist treatment, then neither is concept possession, for recognition is a case of exercising a concept. Once such a breach in the reductive account of intellectual activity has been created there will be no motive for pursuing such an account of thought.

Although the argument which I shall now present follows naturally from what went above, it does not depend on it. That is, I am going to argue that if no behaviouristic theory of perception is correct, then neither is a behaviouristic theory of recognition or conception: the detachment of the consequent requires only that behaviouristic theories cannot cope with perception. It does not require that my reasons for thinking it cannot cope are correct. Therefore, what follows is of interest to anyone who rejects a behaviouristic treatment of perception, on whatever grounds.

The arguments is as follows. Let us assume a non-reductive theory of awareness but a behaviourist theory of recognition. In this case, the standard situation will be tripartite in this way. When someone perceives and recognises an object possessing quality F there will be the F object giving rise to an F-appropriate experience ('seeming to

105

see something F', or 'being presented with an F datum', depending on one's theory of perception) followed by the acquistion of an F-appropriate behavioural disposition. I shall argue that it can be shown that the second stage is redundant if one gives this behavioural account of the third stage. But if the second is removed what remains is a behaviourist theory of perception, which has already been refuted. The behaviourist theory of recognition must, therefore, be false.

Let us suppose that, in a given instance the sequence of events, instead of following the normal pattern

(1) F object → F experience → F disposition

followed instead the pattern

(2) F object → G experience → F disposition

or

(3) F object → no experience → F disposition.

Now I take it that it will constitute a *reductio ad absurdum* of the theory if the subject cannot tell which of the three possibilities has been actualised; this would show that, given stages (1) and (3), (2) is redundant. For if the sense of 'experience' has been so weakened that someone cannot tell, not merely what it is of, but whether or not he is having one, then it has been rendered vacuous. Furthermore, we saw in the argument against behaviourist theories of perception that the point of leaving the notion of experience unreduced was that ostension of predicates in experience was essential to the meaningfulness of language. But if a subject cannot tell what is presented as the content of experience then experience is not fitted to perform such a function.

On this theory how can someone tell that he has an experience, or what its object is? To tell the former he must be able to recognise something as a experience, and to tell the latter he must be able to recognise it as a particular sort of experience; both variants involve recognition of something as being of such and such a type. However, on the present theory that simply comes to acquiring a certain disposition. Thus telling whether one is having the appropriate sort of disposition, as in pattern (1), or something deviant, as in (2) and (3), is simply to acquire again a disposition. Suppose that the subject acquires the same sort of disposition as he had previously; does this indicate that he was having the appropriate sort of experience? Telling what sort of experience he is having consists in acquiring the disposition. It will, therefore, seem to him that he has whatever experience is appropriate to the disposition that he acquires. Subjectively, therefore, the second step in the process becomes irrelevant; it really does not matter, to follow Wittgenstein's image, whether the box is empty, or what sort of beetle it contains (1953, 100). And this is the criterion for the redundancy of the second stage in the process. Therefore it seems that it is impossible to combine a reductive account of recognition with a non-reductive account of experience. The argument actually shows something broader than this, namely that it is wrong to regard the connexion between recognition and experience as contingent, for the same argument would operate against any theory that rested upon such a contingent connexion. Something like the traditional doctrine of the incorrigibility of our knowledge of sense contents must be correct: it must be constitutive of our type of consciousness that, for certain basic cases at least, it follows that if someone believes he recognises a certain quality as an object of his experience, then it is such; and conversely, that if he has an experience of a certain sort and is conscious of it, he will conceptualise it appropriately. This form of non-contingent connexion is not available for someone who accepts the mongrel theory that Ayer recommends: for the connexion between the event of the occurrence of a certain experience and further events of how the relevant body tends to react can hardly be other than a causal and therefore contingent connexion.

7

Matter: turning the tables

I INTRODUCTION

It is generally agreed that material bodies are extended in space; they are three-dimensional objects. In the *Second Meditation* Descartes maintained that being extended was the essence of body, but most philosophers have been inclined to deny that extension alone is what constitutes body, for a body is something more than a bare geometrical figure. A bare geometrical figure is just a volume of empty space, but those spaces in which bodies are located are not empty but *occupied*. A body occupies a space in the sense that while it is located in that space no other material body can be located there: to occupy space is to exclude other bodies. It would seem that bodies must of necessity possess some property or properties over and above their geometrical properties; there must be something further which constitutes their materiality, their power to occupy the space in which they are located.

Locke recognised the need to characterise bodies more fully than they are characterised in Descartes's definition, and he saw that their materiality consisted in their ability to occupy space to the exclusion of other bodies. Consequently he introduced as his other essential and intrinsic characterisation of body the property of impenetrability, which just is the capacity of one body to prevent another body from occupying the space it occupies itself, whilst it occupies that space itself (*Essay*, II, 8, 23).

If we add impenetrability to shape and size, the modes of extension, our conception of body comes to be that of a volume of impenetrability. Most people have felt that this is still an inadequate characterisation of what it is to be a material body, and they point out that impenetrability is a dispositional property only. So, to say that something is impenetrable is to say what it will do or how it will act under certain circumstances, namely when another body of an appropriate sort attempts to occupy the space which it occupies itself. But to say how a thing will sometimes act is not to say what it is − it does not tell us the actual or intrinsic or internal nature of the object which supposedly will so act. It seems that the power, capacity, or disposition of an object to act in a certain way cannot be the whole nature of the object, for that power, capacity or disposition becomes actualised only in those movements when the object is acting in the appropriate way, but the object which possesses the disposition is thought to exist actually and really, and not merely potentially when it stands alone not exercising its disposition and interacting with other objects.

Yet there are those who think that it *is* both coherent and correct to conceive of bodies as volumes of impenetrability − that is, as conglomerations of spatially arranged powers or dispositions. This view has a striking similarity to that of modern science which sees the basic constituents of the material world as being purely dispositional entities which are characterised solely by reference to their ability to act upon and influence things in their vicinity. I shall discuss this view in section 4, but before doing so I shall examine attempts to avoid this purely dispositional conception of body by ascribing further non-dispositional properties to bodies over and above the properties of extension and impenetrability which we have already ascribed to them.

It is worth remarking, as a polemical aside, on Armstrong's attitude to this problem. He is fully aware of the difficulties involved in finding non-relational properties, other than geometrical ones, which it is plausible to impute to matter. He admits that he does not know the answer to this problem but excuses himself 'further consideration of the difficulty, on the grounds that it is a quite separate problem from the problems considered in this book' (1968: 283). In a sense it is a separate problem from that of giving a materialist account of mind; but it is a prior one, not a posterior one, for how can anyone reasonably ask people to accept a counterintuitive account of mind for the sake of furthering the materialist programme when it is uncertain whether there is a coherent concept of matter? We have in Armstrong's attitude to these problems a blatant example of the way in which the fashion for scientific realism obscures first the proper philosophical ordering of problems and consequently the actual situation concerning what is philosophically plausible.

2 SOLIDITY: BY IMPENETRABILITY OUT OF CONFUSION

Those who search for something more categorical than a power or capacity with which to fill the volumes that bodies occupy have often lighted upon the quality of solidity as encountered in tactile experience. Harré, not himself a believer in such a quality, expresses clearly the view of those who do believe in it:

> Solidity is the alleged quality, the possession of which is responsible for the fact that two material things cannot occupy the same place at the same time and is logically connected with impenetrability ... in that the former is supposed to account for the manifestation of the latter. Solidity is supposed to be the permanent state of a thing which ensures that a thing has the secondary power to resist any other body. (1970: 305)

I shall present three arguments against the view that solidity can figure in this way as the qualitative 'filler' of body.

(1) There are two *prima facie* coherent views concerning the relation between the quality solidity and the power impenetrability. First, it might be argued that in touch we experience a certain quality which we find to be possessed by all and only those bodies which resist penetration. This quality we call solidity because it is constantly conjoined with the power of impenetrability. According to this view one could not claim that the quality is identical with the power but only that it is the quality which give evidence of, or is causally associated with, the presence of the power. The second possible view is that in touch we experience the power called impenetrability: it can thus be called a quality in so far as that term simply signifies that it presents itself as a datum in experience. Neither of these two views will help the materialist out of his problems. In the first case, the quality of solidity does not explain or constitute the power to resist penetration; it is merely contingently connected with its presence and therefore it ought to make sense to imagine either without the other: there is no 'internal' connexion between the two features and, so conceived, solidity would be no better a candidate for what actually constitutes materiality than would, for example, colour, realistically interpreted. In the second case, the assertion is simply that at least one type of power can be directly experienced. This claim in no way alters the fact that impenetrability is just a power and that the world being revealed by touch is a world consisting of volumes of impenetrability. As the quotation from Harré suggests, what those who put their faith in solidity are after is both a quality and a power in a sense which means more than that the power is directly experienceable. What is desired is that the quality is a genuine quality, the power a power, and that the two are necessarily

110

connected such that there could not be a quality like that if it were not also a power: the quality entails and therefore explains the power. It is difficult to *prove* that the importation of synthetic necessities into the phenomenal realm in this way is improper. It does, however, look as if this peculiar desired position seems legitimate only because it is a confusion of the other two: the contingently connected quality from the first becomes confused with the directly experienceable power from the second. Put at its weakest, such synthetic necessities should be objects of suspicion.

(2) For any sense, the same informational value could be embodied in a subjectively different type of sense experience. That this is so is attested by the fact that people with very few of our normal physical senses (e.g. a blind, deaf-mute) can come to understand the same theory about the world as we accept. Now consider the following proposition: what one's tactile experience is like — including what the quality of solidity seems to us to be like — is a function of the type of receptors by which we feel; that is, the receptor type is a causally necessary condition for the experience being as it is. If this proposition is accepted — as surely it must be — in company with the proposition that the quality of solidity as presented in touch is a real quality of objects, we must conclude that anyone whose receptors were fundamentally different, such that his experience was subjectively quite different from ours, would not get an accurate idea of solidity even if his idea possessed all the same formal properties (i.e. those relating to the causal properties of the object) as ours. This is no better than the dogma which I shall consider in the next section, that it is reasonable to attribute absolute colour to objects. What is more, this felt solidity is meant not merely to be objective, but also to be the ground and explanation of the dispositional property of impenetrability; but if various receptors and, therefore, various experienced qualities could fill the bill of correlating with these causal powers, and each seem the natural experiential facet of solidity to the observer with the relevant type of sense, how can there be this logical or internal connexion with impenetrability? Are we to believe that the subject with our type of sense really apprehends the connexion directly, though others would merely learn it?

(3) Solidity as given in touch is a property of macroscopic objects and of microscopic ones if one takes a Newtonian corpuscularian view of the 'minute parts'. But it is not a property of the microscopic as that is conceived in modern physics: fields, energy and charges are

not solid. The line of argument developed in (2) already suggests that it is unreasonable to treat sensible qualities as independent of our senses. We can add to this that science has no role for solidity beyond impenetrability. Therefore, if the ontology of modern science is correct, solidity is not an intrinsic feature of matter.

3 SECONDARY QUALITIES AS THE GROUND OF OUR BEING

We remain, therefore, in the position of conceiving of objects as nothing more than volumes of impenetrability. Perhaps we can escape from this 'powers' conception of body by ascribing one of the traditional secondary qualities, realistically conceived, to matter. Colour is the best candidate once tactile sensations have been disposed of, for sounds, tastes and smells are qualities emitted by objects, but colours seem to be qualities possessed intrinsically by them: the colour is where the object is and not something *from* the object. However, colours will not plausibly fill the bill either, for two reasons.

(1) We are searching for some property which will give categorical or substantial existence to material bodies; something which can save them from being mere collections of powers. How plausible is it to regard the substantiality of an object as consisting in and resting upon a volume of colour? If we adopt colour as the categorical element in material substance we will thereby be conceiving of bodies as volumes of colour possessing an overall shape and possessing dispositional properties at every point within that volume, such as to correspond to the forces exercised either by the whole volume or specifically at that point within the volume: these powers will be powers of the volume of colour, which will be the object itself. This theory is bizarre but it is not incoherent. The position is made neither better nor worse by including the other secondary qualities as well as colour.

(2) Second, one might deny that secondary qualities are intrinsic to objects except as powers. If this Lockean position is correct, then the qualities cannot play the role of replacing powers as the most substantial element in body, for they will themselves only be powers. There are at least three reasons for denying that secondary qualities are intrinsic. First, if one rejects naive realism, it will follow that secondary qualities can be intrinsic in objects only at the price of allowing a dual instantiation; behind the red of my sense-datum is the red of a physical object. This dual instantiation is unreasonable in

the case of secondary qualities in a way that it is not for primary qualities for a variety of reasons. One is that secondary qualities are never assigned a causal role (except, perhaps, as affecting minds), such roles always devolving upon the primary features of the world. The postulation of such qualities is, therefore, scientifically otiose. Our second reason for denying objective status to secondary qualities also functions as an additional argument under the first against dual instantiation. Smart has pointed out that secondary qualities do not bear any very essential relation to the primary qualities that underlie them (1963: 70-1). So the light waves that make something appear green or the particles the emission of which from an object make it smell a certain way will not be essentially similar groups, but collections of essentially heterogeneous waves or molecules which happen, because of the structure of our senses, to affect us in the same way. This suggests that the qualities as we sense them are the production of the idiosyncrasies of our senses and not objective features of the world. Finally, the second argument used against the perceivability of solidity works also as an argument against the objectivity of all sensed qualities. If it is the structural features of our experience that determine the usefulness of the senses, not their qualitative ones, and if, therefore, any structurally similar qualities would seem to be equally correct there can be no good ground for attributing the quality as sensed to the external world.

4 POTENTIALITY AND VACUITY

We started with a purely geometrical conception of body; then we filled it with impenetrability. Then, feeling dissatisfaction with such a dispositional filling for the physical cake we tried solidity, hoping that that would act as the ground of the impenetrability. After the failure of this attempt we tried to fill body with colour but found this implausible. Consequently we are left with a conception of body which makes it spatial and dispositional only. This line of reduction of matter to something merely dispositional does not only apply to the Lockean or atomist picture of the physical world. More modern conceptions of matter are overtly and directly dispositional. Nowadays we are presented with an ontology which is avowedly devoid of quality, containing only quantitively discernible forces, fields and energies, all of which are entities existing only as forms of disposition, power and influence. Here we arrive at something of a paradox. On the one hand, those philosophers who, by arguments similar to our own, have reached this attenuated view of matter have tended to fall into idealism, regarding a world of powers as too insubstantial to command belief. On the other hand, this is the theory that physical science advocates. It is, therefore, not surprising that some realist philosophers of science have attempted to defend this etiolated conception of matter. If the arguments in the previous sections of this chapter are sound, the materialist and the non-idealist are obliged, the former to show that the view that there is nothing but such powers is not incoherent, and the latter to show that it is not incoherent to hold that everything material is so constituted. I hope to prove that they both fail to escape from this predicament.

Harré drawing on the theories of the eighteenth century Czech priest and diplomat, Boscovitch, expresses the general form of the powers ontology as follows:

Every fundamental theory must, as expressed in the language of physics, be a field theory. (1970: 313)
The ultimate entities of the world, as we can understand it, must be point sources of mutual influence, that is centres of power distributed in space. They are perpetually redistributing themselves in space, that is, they are continuously changing their spatial relations, and, consequently, their mutual influences, since these are distance dependent. (ibid.: 308)

Unfortunately, little is said about the nature of powers and certain problems and limitations inherent in the notion thereby go neglected. Starting from the intuition that any real entity must possess a determinate nature we can generate an argument against the ontology of powers.[1]

(1) Every real object must possess a determinate nature.

(2) The nature of any power P is given by what would constitute its actualisation.

Therefore,

(3) If P is a real object it must be a power to a determinate actualisation.

(4) As P must have a determinate actualisation and the determinacy of a power rests upon the determinacy of its potential effect (that is, given (1), (2) and (3)) then if a power Q is the actualisation of P, the determinacy of P will depend upon the determinacy of Q; that is, of Q's actualisation.

---

1   The following is, I think, a fuller version of what is suggested in Holt, 1976-7. He argues that 'The idea that "bundles of causes" simply act on other bundles of causes is surely logically insupportable since the notion of any cause is incomplete without the specification of its effect' (p. 23).

It is plain that this principle leads by generalisation to a regress such that

(5) The list of effects constituting the determinate and complete nature of P will be finite only if the list contains (and thereby terminates at) an effect which is not a power.

However,

(6) An infinite list constitutes indeterminacy.

Therefore,

(7) A determinate power must issue at some point in its chain of consequences in an effect which is not itself a power.

It is necessary to clarify the notion of a determinate actualisation, as it relates to powers. What must be determinate is not the general potentiality of a power, but the state brought about by it on any given occasion of its actualisation. Thus it is conceivable that P is the power to make any white thing within six inches of it coloured. This may be a determinable power in that it randomly makes things different colours, and therefore the nature of the power can only be given generically as the power to make them coloured. But in the case of any given actualisation of this power the patient object must become a determinate colour. This is the sense in which a power must be determinate, namely that the state of affairs that constitutes its actualisation in any given case must be a determinate state of affairs.

As a further difficulty, it might be objected that the statement that the actualisation of something consists in a power is itself ambiguous. It might be said the 'The actualisation of P is to produce power Q' suggests that what P produces is some new power state, whereas what it would have to mean to cover the Boscovitchian scheme would be that P is the power to alter the location of Q and that the alteration could be precisely specified; thus it is not the power itself that is altered but only its location. But this answer will not suffice, for it must be possible in principle to specify the state brought about by the power, for the reason given above, and that state is the location at some place *of power* Q. To say that one alters a place is either nonsense or incomplete, for one only alters the place of something, and therefore a specification of what has been moved is essential for a determinate specification of what has been done.

However, it has still not been made clear what counts as an adequately non-potential specification of a state of affairs. Suppose a power to have as its actualisation the production of a change of shape in a certain object, shape being a paradigm of a quality and not a power, and that object possesses a certain power. Would the first power be determinate in virtue of the production of the quality change, or would the possession of the potentiality by the object entail that its determinacy require determinacy of the power of the object, that being part of the total state produced by the initial power? To set the stronger requirement would mean that a world in which all objects possessing qualities also possess powers would be as subject to the regress as a world which consisted solely of powers; and this is counter intuitive. The relevant factor is that feature of the resulting state of affairs which is nomically related to the power; that is, that feature which the power is designated as a power to produce. If this is qualitative then the regress is terminated, unless, as with location, the quality in question can only be completely expressed by reference to something further and that turns out to be a power.

Having explained the argument to (5) we must consider the most crucial controversial premise in the argument, (6). It might be denied that the regress is vicious on the grounds that, at any given step, one can say what the next power is, after a fashion − one merely can never finish the process. However, this cannot be virtuous. If a determinate conception of the power requires the specification of an infinite series of events, it is in principle an incompletable conception; but if a concept is in principle incompletable in this way it is indeterminate. (I said 'incompletable *in this way*' because the incompletability of, for example, *pi* is different, for in that case a definite point is being approached, whereas in the case of the powers it is precisely such a definiteness of end that is missing.) This can be seen intuitively if we consider a regressive specification of a power: P is the power to produce (alter) a power to produce (alter) a power to produce ... Such a formula seems to tell us nothing about what is actually done.

I fear that at this point we shall be faced with objections from the philosophy of allusion and metaphor as practised by some philosophers of science. Using the magical net of holism they will try to fish sense out of a sea of nonsense. We will be told that the absolute interdependence of terms in empirical theory in no way impugns the intelligibility of the overall web of theory, which is self-sustaining, or is sustained by its place in scientific practice. Unfortunately, vagueness is of the essence of this viewpoint and it can, therefore, present no opposition to what I hope are the precise arguments given

116

above. Indeed, the above argument shows that interdependence has its limits. PME showed (in ch. 6.2) that interdependence alone was not enough, requiring also empirical demonstration; the argument above shows that some concepts must not be essentially relative in their characterisation. These theses are not identical for some may hold that certain powers are demonstrable, *qua* powers, although one is likely to hold that the demonstrable and the non-relative are co-extensive. As argued in chapter 5.5 none of this shows that there are concepts which we could have without a framework of grammar — that is another matter — but it does impose constraints on elements within that framework.

The argument, therefore, is sound. We have established that the world of powers is logically dependent on the world (real or potential) of categorical properties — although in nature, of course, the dependence may run the other way, as the actualities depend upon the powers for their generation. But what sort of thing are these actual or categorical entities? According to Harré they are sensible qualities; that is, such things at least as colours, sounds and smells (1970: 303). He is surely right in seeing the sensible qualities as the obvious candidates for actuality: the phenomenal realm is that area which cannot be reduced to potentialities. Bearing in mind the conclusion that we have reached regarding the mind-dependent nature of secondary qualities, we can say that the only categorical entities that can end the regress are mental states with sensible qualities as their objects.

In the context of the overall enterprise of this essay it is worth noticing that this entails that no one who believes that the physical world consists entirely of powers can be a materialist, upon pain of vacuity. For if mental states are only physical and therefore themselves only powers and lacking categorical experiential content the regress could never be terminated. It is indeed a happy coincidence that Armstrong adopts the view that all dispositions must have a categorical base (1968: 86). The arguments of sections 1 — 3 suggest that it is also fortunate for him that he did not try to say what that base could ultimately be. If we take the ontology of modern science, however, to be simply one of powers, it is interesting to note that this is incompatible with a materialist theory of mind.

It seems that determinacy in a power consists in its ability to contribute, directly or at a remove, to mentality. So if all physical entities or properties are ultimately powers it follows that they must

117

all be able, in the appropriate context, so to contribute. This conclusion manages to be, on the one hand, interesting but, on the other, apparently very weak. It is interesting because it gives us a concept of matter analogous to phenomenalism, for it places the essence of matter in its ability to produce experience. It is apparently weak because there would appear to be no physical power which could not, in the appropriate context, causally contribute to mentality. This is so because there is no reason to limit the context to the actual world; that a given power could make the appropriate contribution in some world would be enough to establish its determinacy. But for any given power we could imagine some further powers in the company of which it would produce mentality. There might even, therefore, be a world which did not possess the capacity to produce mental states, but each element in which could so contribute in the context of different powers than those with which it actually shared that particular world. Thus any power, specified according to its physical potentialities after the manner of some scientific theory, will also trivially possess a mental potentiality realisable in some possible world. However, further examination will show that this weakness in our conclusion is apparent only, not real.

We have spoken so far of the requirement that each physical power should be able to make some contribution to the production of mentality. This suggests that the same power has two aspects, one concerned with its physical effects, the other with its mental. But because mentality is a 'dangler', not in any way deducible from physical theory, these two aspects cannot be regarded as functions of the same power, for two ranges of effects can be regarded as effects of the same power only when there is one law or formula which describes both. For example, suppose a field has the power to make an object weighing x lb and situated a in. away move towards the centre of the field at 1 m.p.h.: and also the power to make an object weighing $2x$ lb and $2a$ in. away move at 0.25 m.p.h. In such a case there is one clear formula at work relating distance from the centre, weight and acceleration. But if the laws governing the production of mental states cannot be integrated into those describing the other operations of matter then the mental power cannot be expressed as an aspect of the same power as the other physical powers.

It is important to remember that we are talking here about powers as such and not objects that possess powers. Naturally one object

118

might possess two different powers, but on the ontology we are considering the powers are the only objects and cannot, therefore, be treated as the owners of them: one power, that is, cannot be said to be the owner of two entirely discrete potentialities for two discrete potentialities simply are two powers, not one.

Using M for mental and P for physical we can say that the M power is emergent with respect to the P power. This, however, can be taken in two ways. Given that basic physical atoms contribute to the production of mind only by combining with many other such atoms in very complex structures it might be said that the M power is an emergent property of such complex physical structures; that is, that individual atomic P powers do not have a correlated M power. On the other hand, one might claim that, because each P power can make contributions in different combinations to producing different mental states, it has a correlated M power in its own right. (It would, of course, be a pre-condition for this latter view that the range of contributions to mentality of which the power was capable could be expressed in a systematic way. Otherwise there would be no determinate formula for the atomic M power and the same objection as we raised against consolidating the M and P powers would operate against unifying the atomic M power.) The first alternative is the natural one to choose, for ascribing some M power to each atomic P power as its companion, contingently associated with it, seems bizarre. However, we shall see that our opponent is in fact forced to adopt this remarkable view. For suppose that we choose the first alternative, so that M powers emerge into existence from P powers only when the latter are combined in complex structures. It will follow that the P powers should be able to exist without the M powers and this has already been shown to be incoherent. This follows in virtue of the following general principle: if some phenomenon A is emergent with respect to a realm B then the intelligibility or coherence of B (not merely the being-known of B) cannot rest upon the fact that it produces A. This is so because if A is emergent it is only contingently connected to B and B's internal laws, and being only so connected it can make no essential contribution to the sense or meaningfulness of talk about B.

Referring back to what was proved above, the point can be made in a slightly different form. Avoiding a vicious regress of powers required that any given power be part of a chain of powers which ends in the possible production (as the actualisation of the final

119

power in the chain) of something categorical. But if there is a nomological chasm between the physical and mental no series of physical powers can end in this way, for the production of mentality can never be expressed as an aspect of a physical potentiality.

We can dismiss, therefore, the theory that mental potentiality is emergent with physical complexity; we must choose the other option, namely that mental potentiality exists together with physical at the atomic level. It has already been argued that one single power cannot be both an M and a P power, therefore it follows that there must be two types of basic atom. The question is whether we can characterise their relations and mutual influence in such a way that the ability of the M power to produce actual mental states can bring to an end the regress of P powers. We shall see that this cannot be done.

First, let us notice what a strange world we are postulating. *Prima facie* it is much more natural to think of M power as emerging with physical complexity, for the nature of atomic M powers is extremely opaque. They will not be observable or detectable among P powers for, having no P potential themselves, they could never influence any instrument of observation. We could only tell that they were present when a mental state was produced, and this would not be a means of detecting individual M powers, for more than one would be required to produce a mental state. This follows because if one were sufficient and they existed independently of P power structures, it would follow that all M powers were always producing their appropriate mental state irrespective of whether an appropriate body was present. Assuming that minds exist only in conjunction with bodies of a certain sort it must be the case that the right combination of M powers comes about only as a result of particular combinations of P powers. However, this supposes interaction between M and P powers, in the form of the ability of P powers to determine the combination of M powers and such interaction is not possible. For it to be possible it would have to be the case that M powers could be influenced by P powers. But being influenced by a P power involves a form of P potentiality. This passive power cannot be regarded as an aspect of the mental potentiality and is therefore not a property of the M power. Nor can this passive power of the M power be dismissed on the grounds that it is merely passive and the real potentiality be attributed to the P power that influences it, for even if the effect that P powers had on M powers could be expressed in the same formula as that which described their influence on other P powers (e.g. as the power to change their location in a certain way) this would not of itself wholly explain the influence. There could not be a power which was a power to influence the location of something irrespective of the nature of that thing (though it might be able to influence everything that in fact existed), for natural influence is relative to the nature of the thing influenced. Fire, for example, will only burn what is combustible, and how something is determines whether it will burn just as much as the nature of fire determines whether that thing will burn. Passive potentiality cannot, therefore, be regarded as a mere privation.

On this ground we can say that interaction between pre-existing M and P powers is impossible; therefore neither the emergence of M potentiality nor the pre-existence of M powers infuses content into the notion a physical world consisting entirely of powers.

5 THE LAST DITCH: A NAMELESS RESIDUE

One position remains to someone who believes in matter. He might abandon the ontology of bare powers and give those powers an owner of which we can know nothing. He might, that is, postulate as unknown and in principle unknowable residue which stands to the power rather as a magnet stands to its magnetic field − that is, as something categorical at its centre. This would be rather like Price's spatial occupants (1932: 275ff 14) or the Lockean (or supposedly Lockean) substratum. [2] Such a residue could not, of course, possess any knowable quality for the reasons given above for not allowing qualities to matter. But its nature could be regarded as analogous to an object with sensible qualities. This residue would be a very strange type of entity. Berkeley's scoff at substratum that it is nothing but the bare idea of being itself would be appropriate here: it would be nothing other than the idea of bare physical being. But though the idea might be disreputable it might do to save matter for those who are desperate in that cause. The introduction of a residue, which will be a categorical entity rather than a power, removes the need for the M potentiality, for the actual effect which terminates the regress of powers to affect powers could be the relocation of a categorical residue. The picture of interaction that follows this scheme would be that the P power moved the residual owner of the power (see diagram). As we finally have the owner of powers, the

2   *Essay*, II, 23, 2. For a persuasive statement of the view that Locke did not believe in the substratum see Ayers, 1975.

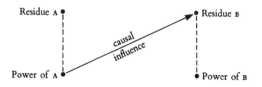

Residue A •   • Residue B

causal influence

Power of A •   • Power of B

absence of which seemed so damaging in previous arguments, the P power can, by moving the residue, move the influences that belong to it.

Whether the postulation of a residue is helpful depends on the relationship that is taken to hold between powerfields and their owners. If an object A possesses a field F and A is moved, is the consequent movement of F a causal consequence of the movement of A, or something stronger? If the movement of F were only a causal consequence of the movement of A then A might have moved and F remained where it was. If we try to avoid this by saying that A has a power to move F, as F itself is a power of A, we are moving along the first steps of a regress. On the other hand, if A moves F, but not by some further power, then the causal connexion between the motions of A and F will be one of bare conjunction; it would be bizarre for someone operating with an ontology in which real potentiality was the only detectable feature to import Humean conjunction in this way. If the residue is to be of any help, therefore, we must be able to regard the connexion between it and the fields of power that it possesses as more than causal. I find this difficult to do, given that the field occupies a different area from that occupied by its owner. The field of a residue, that is, can never be regarded as constitutive of it in the way that, for example, the surface of something can be so regarded. The remaining of the residue or of any field owner in the same intrinsic state (whatever that may be) seems to be compatible with the presence or absence of a given field.

In short, the situation is this. We introduced the residue to be the owner of the power in the belief that the movement of a power would be explained by the movement of the residue to which it belonged and of which it is, in some sense, a property. This seemed a reasonable thing to believe, because it was assumed to be necessarily the case that whenever something is moved so are its properties. However, whilst this applies in an intuitively obvious way to most qualities it is not obvious that it applies to powers. It is not, for example, true of relational properties. An object moved which

122

previously had the property of being two inches away from my hand will probably lose that property on being moved. Although real potentialities are not meant to be purely relational properties, like the spatial relation in our example, neither are they intrinsic to the object in the way that its shape or surfaces or mass are. That is, it makes no sense to suggest than an object might move and leave its shape, surfaces or mass behind it; but it does seem to make sense to think of a magnet being removed and its field of influence remaining, or its field moving away from it. What seems conceivable for the magnet should be conceivable for a residue if that is thought of in the only way it can be, namely on analogy with a quality-possessing centre to a field. It seems, then, that someone who accepts residues must either import bare Humean conjunction to explain their connexion with their powers, maintaining that this counts as more than a coincidental connexion, or think of the fields as essentially tied to their centres in a manner which defies intuition. Whether either of these options really makes sense I would not like to say. I am sure that they represent view-points which no one would happily settle for. But we are now dealing with extremely peculiar and etiolated concepts. For this reason absolute refutation is not possible. But the defence of obscurity and possible, but not demonstrable, vacuity is not a very impressive defence. Only a thin streak of verificationism is required in one's temperament to lead one to lose patience with such a concept of matter. The belief in mind-independent matter turns out to be too unclear to be clearly refuted. Dogmatism has its last ditch; it can be refuted only if it hedges by trying to work a compromise with the demands of intelligibility.

Conclusion

I have tried to show that the principal contemporary forms of materialism are, despite their intellectual sophistication, quite hopeless. However, this essay is not just a survey of heterogeneous philosophical arguments whose only common feature is that they are fashionable and support physicalism. Their connexion is deeper and more systematic.

It is impossible to prove *a priori* that no form of materialism could work. Or perhaps that was proved right at the outset: the argument in the second section of chapter 1 is a perfectly general reason why no materialist theory could be adequate. The materialist theories are all more or less *ad hoc* ways of avoiding this knock-down argument. It is unreasonable to expect anyone to provide a further argument to show that all possible *ad hoc* evasions of the basic argument must be false. Nevertheless, the materialist strategies are systematically related. Given that it is subjectivity that poses the problems for the physicalist, there are only three options open to him. He might deny that subjectivity as normally understood poses any problem for materialism: he might provide a reductive analysis of it in physicalist or topic-neutral terms, or he might deny that it exists. We have discussed all these strategies in (I hope) their most sophisticated forms. It is true that I have not tried to prove that a new variant on these basic strategies could not be developed, but I cannot see what it could be. Any non-reductive theory which is materialist enough to preserve mechanism must lead to epiphenomenalism, as argued in chapter 1. It is difficult to see how analytical reductionism could fail to be a form, or a derivative, of behaviourism, and any such derivative would emphasise the role of either stimulus or response, as do stimulus materialism and the causal theory. Furthermore, if they are to be plausible they must employ the concept of topic neutrality, and we have shown that that concept is seriously flawed. Nor is it easy to see how a reductive theory could avoid the belief theory of perception, for it must reduce our ordinary notion of experience to some

124

other category. Any theory which denied the existence of subjectivity would face the central problem we raised for the disappearance theory. And if there are flaws in the concept of matter all forms of physicalism will be invalidated by them.

The arguments in this essay are not, therefore, *ad hoc*, but cover all remotely plausible materialist strategies.

They do not, of course, cover Nagel's suggestion that what is required is a conceptual breakthrough which will enable us to state materialism in entirely new terms (1974: 446ff). A *deus ex machina* could perhaps still save materialism, but it is difficult to see even vaguely what form such a conceptual breakthrough could take. In some ways Davidson's theory was an attempt to make such a breakthrough, for he hoped to save the phenomena by devising a radical and different conception of event identity. But his attempt failed.

James called materialism a tough-minded theory. We began this essay by wondering why, if this is so, materialists are so often on the defensive in philosophy. The explanation seems to be that though the materialist makes a show of being tough-minded he is in fact a dogmatist, obedient not to the authority of reason, but to a certain picture of the world. That picture is hypnotising but terrifying: the world as a machine of which we are all insignificant parts. Many people share Nagel's fear of this world view, but, like Nagel, are cowed into believing that it must be true (1965: 340). But reason joins with every other constructive human instinct in telling us that it is false and that only a parochial and servile attitude towards physical science can mislead anyone into believing it. To opt for materialism is to choose to believe something obnoxious, against the guidance of reason. This is not tough-mindedness, but a wilful preference for a certain form of soulless, false and destructive modernism.

References

Anscombe, G. E. M. 1968. The intentionality of sensation: a grammatical feature. In *Analytical Philosophy: Second Series*, ed. R. J. Butler, 158-80. Oxford

Armstrong, D. M. 1968. *A Materialist Theory of the Mind*, London
1969-70. Dispositions are causes, *Analysis*, 30, 23-6
1970. The nature of mind. In *Mind-Brain Identity Theory*, ed. C. V. Borst, 67-79. London
1974. Infinite regress arguments and the problem of universals, *Australasian Journal of Philosophy*, 52, 191-201
1978. *Nominalism and Realism*, Cambridge

Ayer, A. J. 1966 His (untitled) contribution to *What I Believe*, ed. G. Unwin, London
1968. *Origins of Pragmatism*, London
1977. *The Central Questions of Philosophy*, London

Ayers, M. R. 1975. Power and substance in Locke, *Philosophical Quarterly*, 25, 1-27

Berkeley, G. The Principles of Human Knowledge. In *The Works of George Berkeley, Bishop of Cloyne*, vol. 2, ed. A. A. Luce and T. E. Jessop, 1949, London

Blackburn, S. W. 1971. Moral realism. In *Morality and Moral Reasoning*, ed. J. Casey, 101-24. London

Block, N. 1978. Troubles with functionalism. In *Perception and Cognition: Issues in the Foundations of Psychology*, Minnesota Studies in the Philosophy of Science, vol. ix, ed. C. Wade Savage. 261-325. Minneapolis

Brentano, F. 1973. *Psychology from an Empirical Standpoint*, London (originally published in German in 1874)

Broad, C. D. 1925. *The Mind and Its Place in Nature*, London

Carnap, R. 1934. *The Unity of Science*, London

Cornman, J. W. 1971. *Materialism and Sensations*, New Haven, Conn.

Davidson, D. 1967. Causal relations, *Journal of Philosophy*, 14, 691-703
1969. The individuation of events. In *Essays in Honor of Carl G. Hempel*, ed. N. Rescher, 216-34. Dordrecht
1971. Mental events. In *Experience and Theory*, ed. L. Foster and J. W. Swanson, 79-101. London
1973. The material mind. In *Logic, Methodology and the Philosophy of Science*, vol. iv, ed. P. Suppes, L. Henkin, A. Joja and Gr. C. Moisil, 709-22. Amsterdam

Dennett, D. C. 1979. *Brainstorms*, Hassocks, Sussex

126

Descartes, R. Meditations on First Philosophy. In *The Philosophical Works of Descartes*, vol. I, ed. E. S. Haldane and G. R. T. Ross, Cambridge, 1911

Farrell, B. A. 1950. Experience, *Mind*, *59*, 170-98

Feigl, H. 1958. The 'mental' and the 'physical'. In *Concepts, Theories and the Mind—Body Problem*, Minnesota Studies in the Philosophy of Science, vol. II, ed. H. Feigl, M. Scriven and G. Maxwell, 370-497. Minneapolis

Feyerabend, P. 1963-4. Materialism and the mind—body problem, *Review of Metaphysics*, *17*, 49-66

   1975. *Against Method*, London

Field, H. 1978. Mental representation, *Erkenntnis*, *13*, 9-61

Fodor, J. A. 1976. *The Language of Thought*, Hassocks, Sussex

Harré R. 1970. *Principles of Scientific Thinking*, London

Healey, R. 1978-9. Physicalist imperialism, *Proceedings of the Aristotelian Society*, *79*, 191-211

Holt, P. J. 1976-7. Causality and our conception of matter, *Analysis*, *37*, 20-9

Huxley, T. H. 1893. On the hypothesis that animals are automata. In his *Collected Essays*, vol. I, 199-250. New York

James, W. 1907. *Pragmatism: a New Name for Some Old Ways of Thinking*, New York

Kim, J. 1966. On the psychophysical identity theory, *American Philosophical Quarterly*, *3*, 227-35

   1976. Events as property exemplifaction. In *Action Theory*, ed. M. Brand and D. Walton, 159-77. Dordrecht

Kirk, R. 1979. From physical explicability to full-blooded materialism, *Philosophical Quartely*, *29*, 229-37

Kripke, S. 1971. Identity and necessity. In *Identity and Individuation*, ed. M. K. Munitz, 135-64. New York

   1972. Naming and necessity. In *Semantics of Natural Languages*, 2nd edn., ed. D. Davidson and G. Harman, 253-355. Dordrecht

Levin, M. E. 1979. *Metaphysics and the Mind—Body Problem*, Oxford

Lewis, D. 1966. An argument for the identity theory, *Journal of Philosophy*, *63*, 17-25

Locke, D. 1971. Must a materialist pretend he's anaesthetised? *Philosophical Quarterly*, *21*, 217-31

Locke, J. *Essay Concerning Human Understanding*, ed. A. C. Fraser, New York, 1969

Lockwood, M. 1981. What was Russell's neutral monism? In *The Foundations of Analytical Philosophy*, Midwest Studies in Philosophy, vol. VI, ed. P. A. French, T. E. Uehling, Jr. and H. K. Wettstein, 143-58. Minneapolis

Mace, C. A. 1948-9. Some implications of analytical behaviourism, *Proceedings of the Aristotelian Society*, *49*, 1-16

Mackie, J. L. 1979. Mind, brain and causation. In *Studies in Metaphysics*, Midwest Studies in Philosophy, vol. IV, ed. P. A. French, T. E. Uehling, Jr. and H. K. Wettstein, 19-29. Minneapolis

Margolis, J. 1978. *Persons and Minds*, Dordrecht
Maxwell, G. 1978. Rigid designators and mind—brain identity. In *Perception and Cognition: Issues in the Foundations of Psychology*, Minnesota Studies in the Philosophy of Science, vol. ix, ed. C. Wade Savage, 365-403. Minneapolis
Mellor, H. 1977. Natural Kinds, *British Journal for the Philosophy of Science*, *28*, 299-312
Nagel, T. 1965. Physicalism, *Philosophical Review*, *74*, 339-56
   1974. What is it like to be a bat? *Philosophical Review*, *83*, 435-50
Peacocke, C. 1979. *Holistic Explanation*, Oxford
Pitcher, G. 1971. *A Theory of Perception*, Princeton, New Jersey
Place, U. T. 1956. Is consciousness a brain process? *British Journal of Psychology*, *47*, 44-50
Price, H. H. 1932. *Perception*, London
Putnam, H. 1975a. Minds and machines. In *Philosophical Papers*, vol. ii, *Mind, Language and Reality*, 362-85 Cambridge
   1975b. The nature of mental states. In *Philosophical Papers*, vol. ii, *Mind, Language and Reality*, 429-40. Cambridge
Quine, W. V. O. 1953. *From a Logical Point of View*, Cambridge, Massachusetts
   1960. *Word and Object*, Cambridge, Mass.
   1977. Facts of the matter. In *American Philosophy from Edwards to Quine*, ed. R. W. Shahan and K. R. Merrill, Norman, Oklahoma
Quinton, A. M. 1973. *The Nature of Things*, London
Robinson, H. M. 1974. The irrelevance of intentionality to perception, *Philosophical Quarterly*, *24*, 300-15
Rorty, R. 1965-6. Mind—body identity, privacy and categories, *Review of Metaphysics*, *17*, 24-54
Ryle, G. 1949. *The Concept of Mind*, London
Searle, J. R. 1981. Analytic philosophy and mental phenomena. In *The Foundations of Analytic Philosophy*, Midwest Studies in Philosophy, vol. vi, ed. P. A. French, T. E. Uehling, Jr. and H. K. Wettstein, 405-23. Minneapolis
Sellars, W. 1965. Scientific realism or irenic instrumentalism. In *Boston Studies in the Philosophy of Science*, vol. ii, ed. R. S. Cohen and M. W. Wartofsky, 171-204. New York
Smart, J. J. C. 1963. *Philosophy and Scientific Realism*, London
Wiggins, D. R. P. 1974. Essentialism, continuity and identity, *Synthèse*, *28*, 321-59
Wilkes, K. 1978. *Physicalism*, London
Wilson, G. 1979. Cheap materialism. In *Studies in Metaphysics*, Midwest Studies in Philosophy, vol. iv, ed. P. A. French, T. E. Uehling, Jr. and H. K. Wettstein, 51-72. Minneapolis
Wittgenstein, L. 1953 *Philosophical Investigations*, trans. G. E. M. Anscombe, Oxford

Index

holism, 92; of mental 27-8
Holt, P. J., 114
Huxley, T. H., 2
idealism, 73-5, 90
identity, mind-brain, 51-3, 61-7;
  necessity of, 60-7; type-token, 25-6,
  58-9
impenetrability, 108, 110-11
inert gas, 11
intentional objects, 6, 70-2
intentionality, 3-4; and perception, 5
interaction, 10, 11, 13, 20
introspection, 39-40; as 'scanning', 52-3,
  67-8, 69-78
intuiting essences, 44-5
inverted spectra, 53-4

James, W., 1, 125

Kim, J., 15-7
Kripke, S., 21, 22-4, 28; and identity,
  60-7

Levin, M. E., 7n, 43, 44-6
Lewis, D. K., 36, 53
Locke, D., 5
Locke, J., 108, 121n
Lockwood, M., 64n

Mace, C. A., 77
Margolis, J., 5
materialism, varieties of, 2-3
matter, 108-23, passim, 125; and
  secondary qualities, 112-13; and
  powers, 108-10, 113-21
Maxwell, G., 64n
mechanism, 1-2, 8-10, 124
mental representation, 4, 58-60
minimal empiricism, principle of, 96-8,
  99, 101, 102, 104, 117
Moore, G. E., 21

Nagel, T., 2, 5, 9, 125
natural kinds, 23
necessity, 20-2; of identity, 60-7
nominalism, 50, see universals
nomological danglers, 8, 118

Ogden C. K. and Richards, I. A., 4

pain, 19, 22-3, 35-7, 44-5, 60-7
Peacocke, C., 10, 13, 20, 22-4, 25, 28, 61
perception, act-object theory, 7;
  adverbial/intentional theory, 5-8, 47;
  belief theory, 69, 74-5, 95-105; direct
  realism, 5-8; and topic neutrality,
  46-50

phenomenalism, 3, 118
Pierce, C. S., 105
Pitcher, G., 95, 100, 102-3
Place, U. T., 6
Plato, 1
powers, see matter
Price, H. H., 121

Quine, W. V. O., 20-1, 97
Quinton, A. M., 5, 76, 77

realism, of properties, 22; of universals,
  46-50
recognition, 105-7
reduction, 5, 6, 9, 10, 20-34 passim, 62,
  79; and functionalism, 29-34, 45; and
  perception, 95-107; and properties,
  18-9; and supervenience, 20-34; and
  translation, 24-7
relativism, conceptual, 90-4
Richards, I. A., Ogden C. K. and, 4
rigid designation, 60-7
Robinson, H. M., 6n
robots, 20, 29-30
Rorty, R., 79-83, 86-9, see also
  disappearance theory
Russell, B., 64n
Ryle, G., 35, 36, 54-5, 67, 77

Searle, J. R., 32
secondary qualities, 'gap' theory, 47, 48,
  49-50; and matter, 112-13
self-consciousness, see introspection
Sellars, W., 80, 88-9
sense-contents, 5, 6, 44, 45
Smart, J. J. C., 28, 35, 37, 38, 40-2, 43,
  44, 46, 47, 85, 113
solidity, 109-12
stimulus materialism, 40-6, 51, 124
supervenience, 20-34 passim; and
  reduction, 20-34; and topic neutrality,
  29-34

theoretical identity, 9, see event identity
topic neutrality, 18, 25-7, 40-2, 52, 62,
  79-80, 124; defined, 41-2; and
  functionalism, 29-34; and perception,
  46-50; and universals, 46-50
Turing machine, 33

universals, 46-50

Wiggins, D. R. P., 64-5
Wilkes, K. V., 19, 29, 32, 86
Wilson, G., 6n
Wittgenstein, L., 82, 107

130

For EU product safety concerns, contact us at Calle de José Abascal, 56–1°,
28003 Madrid, Spain or eugpsr@cambridge.org.